"Sweeney harnesses his gifts as ̠
Elk where he belongs: with the ̠
Christian tradition. A book for ̠
introduction to Black Elk's life or experts looking to see unseen facets
of his witness."

> —Damian Costello, author of *Black Elk: Colonialism and Lakota
> Catholicism*, vice-postulator of the cause of canonization for
> Nicholas Black Elk

"This important, informative book honors the complexities of
conversion and inculturation. It will be an inspiring read for any
spiritual seeker."

> —Julia Walsh, Franciscan Sister of Perpetual Adoration,
> and host of the Messy Jesus Business podcast

"Servant of God Nicholas Black Elk lived a complex life during a
complicated time. Jon Sweeney skillfully relates the monumental cultural
and spiritual losses the Lakota people endured from US governmental
colonialism as he simultaneously traces Black Elk's lifelong quest of the
Holy. From a transcendent childhood vision to a Native healing practice
to Catholic baptism and ministry, Black Elk walked his own 'good red
road' as a Lakota Catholic, integrating both faith traditions into his
spirituality. Readers may come away understanding that this holy
man—who prayed comfortably with both a Rosary and a pipe—well
deserves to be named the first US Native American male saint."

> —Judith Ann Zielinski, OSF, Writer/Producer
> Documentary film *Walking the Good Red Road:
> Nicholas Black Elk's Journey to Sainthood*

"Amid a plethora of diverse and conflicting narratives, author Jon M.
Sweeney presents the rich spiritual legacy of Nicholas Black Elk with
straightforward clarity for novice readers. In so doing, the author draws
upon the scholarship of numerous authors, from Nebraska poet laureate
John G. Neihardt to anthropologist Raymond D. DeMallie and religious
studies scholar Michael F. Steltenkamp, SJ, among others. He deftly
introduces young Black Elk's great childhood vision, his tireless support
for his people's wellbeing, and his lifelong quest to better know and serve
the Great Spirit. With diverse examples, the author explains how Black
Elk embraced Christianity and pursued a robust catechetical career
among his people while grounded in his Lakota culture and identity."

> —Mark G. Thiel, Archivist at Marquette University

People of God

Remarkable Lives, Heroes of Faith

People of God is a series of inspiring biographies for the general reader. Each volume offers a compelling and honest narrative of the life of an important twentieth- or twenty-first-century Catholic. Some living and some now deceased, each of these women and men has known challenges and weaknesses familiar to most of us but responded to them in ways that call us to our own forms of heroism. Each offers a credible and concrete witness of faith, hope, and love to people of our own day.

More titles to follow . . .

Nicholas Black Elk

*Medicine Man,
Catechist, Saint*

Jon M. Sweeney

LITURGICAL PRESS
Collegeville, Minnesota

www.litpress.org

© 2021 by Jon M. Sweeney
Published by Liturgical Press, Collegeville, Minnesota. All rights reserved. No part of this book may be used or reproduced in any manner whatsoever, except brief quotations in reviews, without written permission of Liturgical Press, Saint John's Abbey, PO Box 7500, Collegeville, MN 56321-7500. Printed in the United States of America.

1	2	3	4	5	6	7	8	9

Library of Congress Control Number: 2020943315

ISBN 978-0-8146-4416-4   978-0-8146-4441-6 (e-book)

For my old friend, Peter Dwyer

My friend, I am going to tell you the story of my
        life, as you wish;
and if it were only the story of my life I think I
        would not tell it.

—(Nicholas) Black Elk,
the opening lines of *Black Elk Speaks*
by John G. Neihardt

Contents

Introduction

Imagine you are someone who is passionate about your faith. You probably are if you've turned to a book like this. One day you discover teachings or spiritual practices that are new, as well as appealing, to you. While not obviously kindred to your faith, these new ideas and practices seem applicable. What do you do with them? This is the experience many Christians have when encountering Native American spirituality for the first time. There is a "wow" factor when they discover Indigenous folktales, creation myths, theological ideas, religious rituals and ceremonies—the list could go on. There is a desire to grasp onto these things and appropriate them because they are exciting and rich—and to perhaps even incorporate some into their Christian lives. Is that acceptable? How much of this adopting is appropriate, and at what point does appropriation become usurping and colonizing?

This is the crux of the problem when talking about Black Elk or writing a book about him—a book which mostly Christians will read. It is too easy for Christians to "use" him. It is too common for Christians to take parts of what they discover in someone like Black Elk and leave the rest behind. Then Native people are entitled to feel that, yet again, what is precious to them and what is truly theirs has been taken away.

The best way to avoid such a situation is to tell it straight. So this book will be simple biography, not a work of spirituality. If you came here looking for an introduction to Native American spiritual practices and customs, you've come to the wrong place. You will encounter words, phrases, and practices such as Sun Dance, Ghost Dance, sacred pipe, releasing of the soul, and rites of purification—but they are presented simply to tell the story of the life and afterlife of Nicholas Black Elk.

* * *

As will soon become clear, the potential for misunderstanding goes both ways when it comes to Black Elk. He lived a complicated life as both an Oglala Lakota *wicasa wakan*, or "holy man," and a trained Catholic catechist. He bridged Western and Native religious life in a way that is sure to make people on both sides somewhat uncomfortable. So, just as Native people may feel that the integrity and sanctity of their spirituality and practices are being threatened, Christians can feel the same when faced with someone who, in himself, incorporates Indigenous spiritual traditions into a historical faith that they thought they knew. For all these reasons, we move forward carefully and deliberately.

There is also the issue, best stated up front, of how American colonists, then citizens, filled with purportedly Christian self-justification, hurt the Native Americans whom they came to "save." When Thomas Jefferson was president of the fledgling United States, Black Elk's Lakota occupied much of what we now call Montana, Wyoming, Nebraska, and all of North and South Dakota, as well as parts of

Manitoba and southern Saskatchewan in Canada. "Lakota" means "friends or allies," which was the aim of the various Lakota tribes who went by the name, even though it wasn't always the reality. There are seven bands or subtribes of Lakota, of which the Oglala are the majority. They all lived on the vast Great Plains for centuries before European settlers arrived on the continent's eastern shores and eventually began exploring west. There were millions of Native people hundreds of years ago. No one knows for sure how many. The US census of 2000 revealed 108,000 US residents identifying as Lakota, most living on the Pine Ridge Reservation in the southwest corner of South Dakota, on the border with Nebraska. It's White Christians who put them there, of course, on "reservations." Before then, Christians lied to them, stole from them, tricked them, destroyed their way of life (often intentionally), and subjected them to a variety of humiliations. Pine Ridge was established in 1889.

Today we teach our children the myth of the first Thanksgiving, as if the arrival of Europeans on the shores of North America led, most of all, to peace between peoples celebrated over roast turkey and grandmother's stuffing. Is it still necessary to say that this is not so? I think it is.

* * *

There is also the issue of a famous, often confusing, book that has made millions of people think they understand Black Elk. I'm talking about the most popular book ever written about a Native American: *Black Elk Speaks: Being the Life Story of a Holy Man of the Oglala Sioux as told through John G. Neihardt*, first published in 1932. Some have called it an autobiography, including Neihardt himself, but if that's the case it is an accounting of the life of Black

Elk that excludes the most important aspect of more than half his lifetime. The millions of people who have read *Black Elk Speaks* might never discover how he converted to Catholicism—and why—and what a profound impact this had on the second half of his life. For this reason and more, twenty or so years ago the editor of *The Black Elk Reader* opened his introduction with this sentence: "The more we learn about Black Elk, the more controversial he becomes."[1]

You've already seen, a few pages above, the opening lines of this book, which I hope you now will reread more ironically: "My friend, I am going to tell you the story of my life, as you wish; and if it were only the story of my life I think I would not tell it."[2] What Black Elk, whom we know today as Nicholas Black Elk, had to tell John Neihardt was much more than the story of his own life. It was the story of his people: the Lakota Sioux and his people in the church—even though that part didn't make it in.

Neihardt was the poet laureate of Nebraska in 1930 when he traveled to Pine Ridge Reservation in South Dakota to find Black Elk—or someone, anyone, like him. Neihardt conducted three weeks of interviews with his subject in the spring of 1931, suspecting that he'd have an incredible tale to tell—of a living icon of the tears and epic struggle of the Native peoples of the Americas. He depicted in colorful detail how Black Elk grew up on the Plains as second cousin to the famous Crazy Horse. At ten, Black Elk was at the Battle of Little Bighorn and saw what happened. He then became a Ghost Dancer among his people. Stories of ghost dancing were at the heart of what Neihardt wanted from him. Black Elk fought among his people in many of the battles that led to the Massacre at Wounded Knee. There was an exoticism to the tale Neihardt wanted to tell, of what had been lost, perhaps forever.

Most of all, Neihardt wanted to paint a portrait of lost spiritual and religious treasures in Native life. Lost dreams, a vision destroyed. He had an agenda, as every writer does, even those seeking a simple interview. He was writing epic poems about Native American ways, and he wanted to understand the Ghost Dance, what he called the song of the messiah.[3] Black Elk was his opportunity to do that. Neihardt likely invented some of what his subject speaks in the famous book, but we'll go on quoting it anyway, supplementing it with many other sources.[4]

Why is all of this important? The Black Elk that Neihardt preserved is the image that remains in the popular imagination: a lost warrior, a spiritual sage of a once proud people. Scholar of Catholicism and Lakota ways Damian Costello describes it as "the essentialist Black Elk: the proud, defiant, yet vanquished warrior."[5] That's the person Neihardt went looking for when he knocked on the front door of the Pine Ridge Agency in 1930, and as a result, that's what he found. He missed a great deal—some say intentionally so. He wrote in his original preface that Black Elk "seemed . . . to represent the consciousness of the Plains Indian."[6] Such statements are dreamy, indefinable, and yet powerfully appealing to readers hungry for spiritual understanding—and perhaps weary of traditional Western Christianity.

And as I said, every writer has an agenda. I'm sure that I do, too. Another agenda is the one portrayed by Native Americans who want to use Black Elk to support their causes of Indigenous resistance, most recently, in 2016, in the protests in North Dakota over a pipeline at Standing Rock. Sioux author and professor Nick Estes, for instance, blamed Neihardt for using Black Elk, but then also assumed that Black Elk became a Catholic only "to protect himself and his family."[7] This is just as common of a trope about our subject as the tale that Neihardt told of a lonely, sad Indian who had lost everything that mattered to him.

The Great Depression was just beginning when Neihardt traveled to Pine Ridge. There was a crisis of meaning throughout America and the world. World War I had disillusioned Europeans; it took the Great Depression to do the same here. The American Dream was suddenly seen to be a fantasy. It had crumbled. Perhaps a lost civilization provided a key. Also at work in 1930 and even more so when Neihardt's book appeared in 1932 was the sculpting of Mount Rushmore eighty miles northwest of Pine Ridge, still in the Black Hills (*Paha Sapa*, in Lakota). Sculptor Gutzon Borglum was hard at work creating the faces of George Washington and Thomas Jefferson, each the size of ten men, on a mountain once called, in Lakota, "The Six Grandfathers," now baptized "Mount Rushmore" for the New York lawyer who donated $5,000 toward Borglum's work. The White man was imprinting his gods on the face of the mountains of the people whose land they'd recently stolen. For many, Rushmore is a monument to their pain. As Estes has put it, "Each president—Washington, Jefferson, Lincoln, and Roosevelt—had participated in Indigenous genocide and land theft."[8]

Most important to realize is the misunderstanding about Black Elk's life that Neihardt's book leaves behind. Millions of readers have, for decades now, been left with the impression that *Black Elk Speaks* offers a complete portrait. In fact, it leaves out much from Black Elk's final four decades, including every aspect of his Catholic family, his Catholic formation, and his life as a would-be Catholic saint. Kin to this confusion is the mistaken notion that Black Elk sat for those interviews as an old man at the end of life—a confusion fostered by Neihardt's repeated statements at the time about Black Elk's physical blindness. The suggestion wasn't true. Black Elk lived another nineteen years and, as you will soon see, he made clear statements in those nineteen years about how certain people had mis-portrayed him and how his life was about much more.

So despite the fact that *Black Elk Speaks*, after initially poor sales, became "one of the twentieth century's most important documents on Native American culture and . . . a classic of world literature," we must realize that its author neglected to tell a vital part of Black Elk's story: his Catholicism.[9] Neihardt the poet seems to have assumed that the White man's religion was inessential to the true spirit of his Lakota ghost dancer. This is just one of the reasons why later editions of the book changed the cover from "as told to" to "as told *through*" Neihardt.

The book became an international sensation in the 1960s, translated into many languages. The defiance of *Black Elk Speaks* became most popular at precisely the time when the mighty invading US military was suffering defeat after defeat at the hands of the humble Indigenous people of Vietnam. Neihardt was also a charismatic figure, and another stimulus for his book becoming a bestseller was an appearance by him, at the age of ninety-one, on The Dick Cavett Show in 1971. Cavett later wrote his memories of that day:

> As taping went on, I could see the profound effect he was having on bystanders in the studio as he wove his tales and stories in that mesmerizing way of his, taking you back in time. He told his immortal story of Black Elk and the vision this mystic and noble American Indian had so fortunately settled upon Neihardt as the man with the skills and understanding to bring his colorful and spiritual vision to the world.

The TV personality then concludes:

That same post-Neihardt next morning, in New York City, my producer's wife found herself among about twenty people outside the big bookstore across from Carnegie Hall, waiting for it to open. When it did, they all went to the yard-high stack of *Black Elk Speaks* the canny owner had put on display, having seen the show the night before. She bought her copy and then watched as the stack went down, one by one, to zero.

Neihardt had come to embody that essentialist aura that he had once given to his famous subject, and "a book decades old was re-born."[10]

But Robert M. Utley, a former chief historian of the National Park Service and an authority on Sitting Bull, wrote that Neihardt, like Mari Sandoz, who authored a biography of Crazy Horse, and Stanley Vestal, who wrote on Sitting Bull, were three literary scholars of a particular generation who presented themselves inaccurately as historians, "in works that are good literature but bad history."[11] We'll leave it there.

* * *

Black Elk's passionate involvement in historic Catholicism would have dampened the message of any mythic portrayal of a saddened, aging Lakota who had seen his people humiliated, the Plains decimated, and a pristine nomadic way of life gone forever. A Native man teaching the Gospel in a church was not the picture a mythmaker wanted to paint.

The first half of Black Elk's life, as you will read here, does not differ greatly from what you might have read in previous books. But, for the second half of Black Elk's story, you must meet Jesuit priests who were Black Elk's friends, both before and after his conversion. You need to hear about

St. Agnes Chapel, where Black Elk first assisted at Mass, and how he became a catechist. You'll also encounter Our Lady of the Sioux, a small Catholic church in Oglala, South Dakota, and the Pine Ridge Reservation, where "Nick" Black Elk (as he came to be known) died and where many of his extended family still live. The people of Pine Ridge know the whole Black Elk—not simply the Oglala dreamer (chapter 3), the man of adventure and travel (chapter 4), the wise medicine man of their tribe (primarily chapters 3 and 7), but also the Catholic convert, catechist, and missioner (parts II and III).

Finally, this story wouldn't be complete without looking closely at the cause for canonization that is now underway for Nicholas Black Elk. It began in the fall of 2016, first by petition from his great-grandchildren to the Bishop of the Diocese of Rapid City, South Dakota, and then moved forward a year later when Bishop Robert D. Gruss took the case to a vote among the United States Conference of Catholic Bishops in Baltimore, where it was easily approved. Nick Black Elk lived an exemplary life of Christian virtue, bringing hundreds to the faith by his witness and example. As Bishop Gruss explained to the USCCB, he became "an icon who reveals what God calls all of us to be—people of faith and hope, and a source of hope for others."[12]

Basic Chronology

1866*   Born beside the Little Powder River in Wyoming, near the border where Wyoming and Montana meet. A few months later the Red Cloud War (also known as Powder River War) begins, with Native tribes banding together to attack US garrisons.

1868   Fort Laramie Treaty establishes the Great Sioux Reservation, bringing an end to Red Cloud's War. The Black Hills remain the property of Lakota and other nations, but Red Cloud begins to take more government assistance and his leadership of the Lakota dwindles.

1871–75   Black Elk has mystical experiences—preeminently his Great Vision—that mark him as more than the son and grandson of a medicine man but as a genuine future religious leader.

---

* Precise dates were not always kept. We will follow the dating as calculated by Mark G. Thiel and others at Marquette University Special Collections and Archives, home to the Michael F. Steltenkamp, SJ, Papers.

1876 (June 25–26)

> At ten, fights in the Battle of the Little Bighorn—the battle in which Lt. Colonel George Custer dies—and kills three men. His cousin Crazy Horse is the Lakota war hero that day.

1877   With other Oglala, flees to Canada to be near Sitting Bull.

1878   Pine Ridge Indian Reservation established in southwest South Dakota territory.

1880–81   Leaves Canada, returning to the land of his birth and his people, and soon begins his own medicine man practice.

1882   Now sixteen, settled in the Great Sioux Reservation, which soon becomes Pine Ridge Agency and Reservation.

1886 (Nov.)–88

> Joins William "Buffalo Bill" Cody's Wild West Show troupe, traveling to New York, London, Paris, and other cities.

1887   Dawes Act passed. Holy Rosary Mission established by the Jesuits at Pine Ridge Reservation.

1892   Marries Katherine ("Katie") War Bonnet, a Catholic convert. Together they have three sons.

1903   Katie dies.

1904 (Dec. 6)

> Embraces Catholicism with the encouragement of and after studying with Fr. Joseph Lindebner, SJ. Takes baptismal name Nicholas, probably

because it is St. Nicholas's feast day. Thereafter known as Nicholas (or "Nick") Black Elk.

1905   Marries again, Anna Brings White, who is also a Catholic convert.

1907   At forty-one, begins his catechetical ministry, supervised by Jesuits at Pine Ridge. Meanwhile, continues to be involved in Lakota life, celebrations, and rituals.

1931 (May 10–30)
    Interviewed by John D. Neihardt, resulting in the book *Black Elk Speaks*, which eventually becomes a worldwide bestseller.

1934   Writes letters confirming his Catholic beliefs after confusion over *Black Elk Speaks*. In one letter, disavows the book since Neihardt made no mention of his conversion to Catholicism.

1942   Wife Anna dies.

1950 (Aug. 17)
    Nicholas Black Elk dies.

1961   *Black Elk Speaks* is republished and finds a vast international audience, creating an icon out of Black Elk.

2012   St. Kateri Tekakwitha (d. 1680) becomes first Native American to be declared a saint by the Roman Catholic Church.

2016 (Mar. 14)
    Grandchildren of Nicholas Black Elk present petition to Bishop Robert D. Gruss of the Diocese

of Rapid City, South Dakota, asking him to open a cause for canonization for Nicholas Black Elk.

2017 (Oct. 21)

Bishop Gruss, after consulting with the United States Conference of Catholic Bishops, officially opens the cause for canonization of Servant of God Nicholas Black Elk. It is sent to the Vatican.

PART ONE

MEDICINE MAN

CHAPTER ONE

A Place Now Known as Oglala, South Dakota

Black Elk was born in 1866 in what is now the state of Wyoming but was then simply Lakota territory, recently taken from the Crow. It was where Montana and Wyoming come together today at right angles on their southeastern and northeastern edges around the Little Powder River. To the west are Bighorn Mountains and to the east, the rolling Black Hills. That name, in fact, comes from the Lakota. *Paha Sapa* ("Black Hills"), they called them, probably because the mountains were so covered with pine trees that they appeared dark as night from a distance.

The Lakota sometimes shared and sometimes dominated this land. When they shared it, there were Pawnee, Crow, and Cheyenne nearby. Native people have lived on the Great Plains for at least ten thousand years. The Lakota were relatively recent: they seem to have settled there sometime during the eighteenth century. At that time, they knew little to nothing of the new American colonies of Europeans who'd recently landed on the continent's far eastern shores; and those Europeans knew nothing of the Lakota.

3

French Canadian explorers were the first Whites* to travel west of the Mississippi River. They were soon mapping the course of the Missouri River, which lies west of the Mississippi, beginning in western Montana, flowing east, then south through the Dakotas, to the east of where the Black Hills lie. They were looking for new routes for their booming business in animal pelts. There were many animals to be pelted in such a wide wilderness, as well as a hungry market for the skin and fur back in Europe. Then came the Louisiana Purchase of 1803, when President Thomas Jefferson bought 829,000 acres from the citizens of France, including land from the mouth of the Mississippi at *La Nouvelle-Orléans* (New Orleans), all the way up to the Canadian border, including those Black Hills. Explorers and traders began to come in greater numbers, then, and Native people even began to rely on those traders for the goods they brought with them: for example, utensils and firearms, the latter of which were increasingly important, as one tribe wouldn't want to be without what another tribe had come to possess.

For a time, after Jefferson's Louisiana Purchase, the US government spoke of a "Permanent Indian Frontier" to the west of it. There was a sense that US expansion had gone as far as it would go and that Native people would be able to remain autonomous and free, if only on lands to the west of what they had once known. President Andrew Jackson's infamous forced removal of tribes in the east—the Trail of Tears—was the fruit of this policy. This was when sixty thou-

---

* "Whites" is a troublesome and indeterminate term but one I've decided to use because it remains common in both popular and scholarly literature on Native Americans and the taking of their lands. Sometimes I use "Euro-Americans" instead.

sand Indigenous people were forcibly expelled from their ancestral lands in the southeastern United States to lands west of the Mississippi. Then came the Mexican-American War of 1846–48, after which expansion all the way to California and the Pacific Ocean became rapidly inevitable.

The precise date of Black Elk's birth doesn't matter in Lakota tradition, but it's usually remembered by Whites as December 1. John Neihardt recorded the birth as December 6 in *Black Elk Speaks*, based on what he heard from his subject, but that's because he wasn't paying attention to his subject's Catholicism. Such a specific Gregorian calendar date was how Nicholas Black Elk used to describe, not his original birth, but the day he was reborn as a Catholic. December 6 is the feast of St. Nicholas of Myra. It was on some other day, thirty-eight years earlier, in 1866, when a baby boy was named, in Lakota, *Hehaka Sapa*, "Black Elk." He came from a lineage of medicine men. His father, also Black Elk, was both a medicine man and a warrior.

There was much talk, then, among the Lakota about the White kingdom in the east and the threat it was increasingly posing to Lakota ways of life. In the same year Black Elk was born, Red Cloud's War—also sometimes called the Powder River War—began, as the ascendant Oglala chief Red Cloud led his people, together with the Cheyenne and Arapaho, against garrisons recently established by the US government. One conflict of that two-year war came to be known as Fetterman's Massacre, because all eighty-one men under the command of Captain William Fetterman were killed just before Christmas 1866 by Red Cloud and others, including a young Crazy Horse. Fetterman's was the worst defeat of Whites at the hands of Indigenous people on the continent up to that point, and it bookended the great defeat to come at Little Bighorn a decade later.

The existential threat of European settlers had pushed the Lakota and other tribes further and further west, seeking unencumbered land. Whites were continuing to arrive, looking for gold, finding it first in Georgia in 1828 (which helped spur the Trail of Tears), then in the Sierra Nevada of California in 1848, and again five years later in southern California and Montana, prompting some of those settlements and garrisons that Red Cloud attacked.

Even before the gold, there was a drive to seek the "New Eden" that God had supposedly given to the new Americans, according to the popular view. "God hathe hereby cleared our title to this place," wrote one prominent seventeenth-century Massachusetts Bay Puritan.[1] The Massachusetts Bay Company seal of 1775 even featured a Native man in its center, holding bow and arrow, wearing what could be described as fig leaves, saying: "Come over and help us." It didn't hurt that this Edenic land was also rich in resources for plundering; "teeming" is a common adjective in many of the early accounts of White settlers and missionaries alike, for the pelts, the fish, and the buffalo they found.

In 1858, gold was discovered near Pike's Peak in the Kansas Territory (now twelve miles west of Colorado Springs), and for the next three years an astounding one hundred thousand or more White "explorers" rushed over and through Lakota land with their horses, picks, shovels, families, and rifles. Just imagine those feet, carts, and hoofs trampling back and forth over Native lands. It is estimated that half of the gold rushers returned from where they'd come within a single year. One recent history explains: "The two-way mass migration left behind wrecked river valleys with pulverized banks almost devoid of game, grass, and timber."[2]

Pike's Peak is 425 miles due south from where Black Elk was born. Directly west of there, miners with names like Bozeman (John M.) were also finding gold in the Montana

Territory. The trampling continued. Driving the settlers' desire for new places and fresh opportunities were other factors: economic hardship, droughts and environmental disasters, and a gritty determination to survive. There was, for instance, a nationwide economic depression in 1837, when US states didn't extend beyond Missouri. Journalist Horace Greeley wrote at that time: "Fly, scatter through the country, go to the Great West, anything rather than remain here."[3] They did.

Another economic depression came in 1869 and carried through into the early 1870s, prompting more foreclosures and settlers moving west. Their virtue of self-reliance, perhaps praiseworthy on the face of it, had also the vice of denigrating and debasing other people—the Natives whose land and rights they disregarded. The American ethos is built on this. For example, one of our most popular legends, the one created by Laura Ingalls Wilder with her *Little House on the Prairie* books, is founded on the myth that Laura's hardworking Pa owned the land he was fighting for. He didn't. Even the 1870 census taker knew better, writing this in his ledger under the heading "Property Value": "Lands belonged to the Osage Indians and settlers had no title to said Lands."[4]

When Black Elk was born, his people didn't have much of a chance.

* * *

He had eight siblings, all but two of whom were older. He was cousin to the famous Oglala Lakota warrior, Crazy Horse, who was a generation older than Black Elk. Their fathers shared a grandfather. Given the Lakota's reverence and reliance on the animals, "a name that included 'horse' . . . signified strength of character."[5] Crazy Horse was the hero of both of their generations.

Oglala culture centered around many ideas and practices wise and valuable. These earth-honoring ways were as yet undiscovered by Euro-Americans, who customarily believed there was no such thing as Native American civilization— that their life was not cultured but stunted and static. We wouldn't come to think of culture in the plural until the birth of cultural anthropology in the late nineteenth and early twentieth centuries.

This is one reason why the idea also persisted—and still persists in some quarters—of a "Lost Race" predating Native Americans on North American soil. Some of these theories suggest that these tribes were ancient Greeks, Romans, Persians, or Hebrews. The Book of Mormon, the Church of Latter-day Saints' holy scripture, is the most enduring remnant of this thinking. Others posited that early medieval Vikings ruled the land at one time.

The Oglala culture into which Black Elk was born was rich in ways of honoring the land and preserving it. Animals were respected, even when they had to be killed for food and clothing. Still, Oglala culture could be horribly violent in human relationships. Despite the romance of films like *Dances with Wolves* (1990), a fictional blockbuster set among Lakota in the 1860s, in which violence among Native people was employed only when necessary, wars and bloody conflicts with other tribes were routine. Scalping, decapitation, slavery, even cannibalism, were common in the pitch and anger of battle. Women often grieved the loss of their men or children by cutting themselves. Life was bloody, even before there was conflict with White settlers. These behaviors shocked Whites, even as those same Whites failed to recognize the grave moral failings of their own horribly violent actions toward people whom they assumed to be less than human.

Throughout Black Elk's childhood White settlers rapidly moved onto his people's land, forcing the Oglala to relocate to what was being called "reservations" or set-aside lands. The very first such "reservation" was created in 1758 in the soon-to-be state of New Jersey. By 1824, US President James Monroe established an Office of Indian Affairs for the growing problem of where to put Natives whom the US citizenry felt needed to be removed from land the Natives had once occupied. More reservations followed, and of course, they continue to today. Revealingly, the Office of Indian Affairs was then a division of the US Department of War.

Buffalo herds were greatly diminished when Black Elk was a boy, and they were soon to fall away completely. The great creatures were hunted for centuries by the Lakota and other tribes in ways that honored the animals and maintained their presence on the Great Plains. "The buffalo followed the stars, and the people followed the buffalo," as Nick Estes has recently put it.[6] By contrast, in a short amount of time Whites hunted them ferociously, rapidly diminishing their numbers. Then Whites realized that eliminating buffalo from the land would help eliminate the Native people, as well.

For example, in 1883, a young and successful New Yorker named Teddy Roosevelt traveled west by train for a buffalo hunt. Federal programs encouraged such hunts—mass slaughters—as a strategy to rid the Plains of Indians. Parties of recreational hunters would gather in and around the Badlands, drink, and shoot. Passengers on the Northern Pacific Railroad even "blazed away at whatever beasts wandered near the tracks." Teddy Roosevelt's biographer tells these stories as part of the life of adventure in the "Wild West" of the soon-to-be governor of New York and then president of the United States.[7] Likewise, these settlers felled millions of trees across the territories, clearing forest for their new homesteads and farms. Environmental repercussions followed this, including serious drought, followed by massive prairie fires and locust swarms of biblical proportions. (The locust plague of 1875, which devastated the western United States, remains the worst natural disaster the country has ever seen.)[8]

One Native writer, Luther Standing Bear, wrote this, remembering what he saw in the late 1870s as a boy: "Our scouts, who had gone out to locate the buffalo, came back and reported that the plains were covered with dead bison. These had been shot by the White people. The Indians never were such wasteful, wanton killers of this noble game animal. We kept moving, fully expecting soon to run across plenty of live buffalo; but we were disappointed. I saw the bodies of hundreds of dead buffalo lying about, just wasting, and the odor was terrible."[9] This was after smallpox, brought by Whites from Europe, had already killed hundreds of thousands of Indians.

Not all Whites ignored the harm being done to Native people. For example, the first Episcopal bishop of Minnesota, Henry Benjamin Whipple, counseled President Abraham Lincoln in 1862 on the devastation being wrought in Indian communities by national policies. Whipple was hated by many Whites for his stance. And Henry David Thoreau, a year before he died, traveled to the north woods of Minnesota to see Indigenous communities for himself. He seems to have met the chief Little Crow and wrote in his journal of Little Crow and the others: "They were quite dissatisfied with the white man's treatment of them, and probably have reason to be so."[10] But these were the outliers.

CHAPTER TWO

Little Bighorn

Two sets of dates—important to the story of White settlers displacing Native Americans from their land on the Great Plains—are central to the story of Black Elk's first twenty-five years of life. This chapter is about the first of these two.

Little Bighorn, Black Elk Age Ten

The first of these is June 25–26, 1876. Black Elk is only ten years old when, straddling several miles of the Little Bighorn River in what is now Big Horn County, Montana, the Battle of the Little Bighorn (or Battle of the Greasy Grass, as it is known to the Lakota) takes place. This is when the Lakota were victorious over the White invaders on their land and where the famous/infamous Lt. Colonel George Armstrong Custer died.

Imagine that you have a pen in your hand and you begin to draw a wobbly line up and down on a blank piece of paper, the line meandering its way slowly from one top corner of the paper to the bottom corner at the other end. That is pretty much what the usually quiet Little Bighorn

River looks like on a map, moving through canyons, hills, and cutting across the grassy steppes.

Custer, who the Lakota called "Long Hair" for his well-coiffed and easily recognized blonde mane, lived with a reckless bravery that earned him promotions during the American Civil War. He had set out two years earlier from Fort Abraham Lincoln (Bismarck, North Dakota) with more than one thousand men traveling on more than one hundred wagons, "accompanied by a sixteen-piece brass band riding white horses" to explore the previously uncharted Black Hills region of southwestern South Dakota and southeastern Montana.[1]

> What a flamboyant, outrageous figure. What a sense of himself he had. He must have considered himself immortal, at least when his hair was long.

So Custer is described by Evan Connell in one of the most-read books about Little Bighorn ever published, *Son of the Morning Star*.[2]

The campaign that began at Fort Lincoln in early July 1874 traveled straight west through Dakota Territory, steering clear of the Great Sioux Reservation running parallel to the south. It eventually crossed the north-south running Little Missouri River, into Montana Territory towards the Yellowstone River, which the Seventh Cavalry then followed southwest to Rosebud Creek. From there, it was another fifty miles or so further to the southwest, to near the place where the Little Bighorn River splits off from the Bighorn River. They were looking for gold all along the way.

By the standards of the day, Custer wasn't a bad man. Just a few years earlier, for instance, his Seventh Cavalry was in Kentucky beating back Ku Klux Klan activity. There,

they also broke up illegal distilleries. Then c
Chicago Fire and Custer and his cavalry were
the Windy City to help restore order and reb
termath of that disaster.

It doesn't seem that Custer malevolently set out with the
intention of killing Indians, but he believed Native people
could and should live among Whites, writing naively in his
1874 memoir, *My Life on the Plains*: "If I were an Indian I
often think that I would greatly prefer to cast my lot among
those of my people who adhered to the free open plains,
rather than submit to the confined limits of a reservation,
there to be the recipient of the blessed benefits of civilization."[3] Custer was writing at a time when Native war practices—both true and exaggerated—including scalping, scalp
dances, and torture of prisoners, were often told.

Upon arriving in the Black Hills, Custer and his cavalry
regiment either found gold or were rumored to have found
it, and news and photographs of this (more than one pho-
tographer traveled with the Seventh) caused a rush of White
people to the region. They would be done before 1875 was
over—but only to return again in the new year. Their mission was to locate the ideal spot for a military outpost in
the Black Hills and to remove, forcibly if necessary, any and
all Native people who were living on land apart from their
US-government-appointed reservations.

A still diffident, very young Black Elk was present at the
Battle of Little Bighorn, but the battle was led by Crazy
Horse, as well as the legendary Chief Gall. Crazy Horse
remains shrouded in mystery as a historical figure, as one
of the few famous Native men who avoided being photo-
graphed throughout his life. There are a few photos that
have claimed to have captured him, but none did so con-
clusively. He was the hero of the Lakota that day. More than

any other, it was Crazy Horse who strategized and fought for Custer's demise. This paragraph and a half from the classic account from a Lakota's perspective, *Bury My Heart at Wounded Knee*, explains it best:

> For a long time Crazy Horse had been waiting for a chance to test himself in battle with the Bluecoats. [H]e had studied the soldiers and their ways of fighting. Each time he went into the Black Hills to seek visions, he had asked Wakantanka to give him secret powers so that he would know how to lead the Oglalas to victory if the white men ever came again to make war upon his people. Since the time of his youth, Crazy Horse had known that the world men lived in was only a shadow of the real world. To get into the real world, he had to dream, and when he was in the real world everything seemed to float or dance. In this real world his horse danced as if it were wild or crazy, and this was why he called himself Crazy Horse. He had learned that if he dreamed himself into the real world before going into a fight, he could endure anything.
>
> On this day, June 17, 1876, Crazy Horse dreamed himself into the real world, and he showed the Sioux how to do many things they had never done before while fighting the white man's soldiers. When Crook sent his pony soldiers in mounted charges, instead of rushing forward into the fire of their carbines, the Sioux faded off to their flanks and struck weak places in their lines.[4]

Like many Native leaders, Crazy Horse was guided by a vision he had, which told him how he would be safe in battle. Black Elk, himself formed by visions, explained:

> Crazy Horse dreamed and went into the world where there is nothing but the spirits of all things. That is the real world that is behind this one, and everything we see here is some-

thing like a shadow from that world. He was on his horse in that world, and the horse and himself on it and the trees and the grass and the stones and everything were made of spirit, and nothing was hard, and everything seemed to float. His horse was standing still there, and yet it danced around like a horse made only of shadow, and that is how he got his name. . . . It was this vision that gave him his great power, for when he went into a fight, he had only to think of that world to be in it again.[5]

Crazy Horse came late into the fray that day. The battle was already underway while Crazy Horse decorated himself in war paint. He waited to charge until after Custer's cavalry's Winchester rifles had done much of their firing. There are many exhaustive, blow-by-blow accounts of what happened that day. This is not that sort of history, so we won't recount each of the maneuvers and casualties here. But exponentially more White soldiers died than Lakota. Native losses were less than fifty men; the Whites suffered nearly ten times that many—more than in any battle with Indians since Fetterman's Fight, led by Red Cloud and a much younger Crazy Horse, ten years earlier. Also important for history, the reporters who traveled with the garrulous, fame-seeking Custer rapidly published the details of what happened. Headlines quickly appeared in nearly every newspaper around the world with several inches of type: "CUSTER DEAD" and "MASSACRE BY INDIANS." One expert has recently said, "It still stands as the greatest defeat of the U.S. military on American soil of all time."[6]

In the fight, as in every big and small battle that took place on Native lands during Black Elk's youth, "Lakotas were fighting for survival, to protect the bison and their sovereignty, but they were also fighting to keep alive a broader vision of America where coexistence through right thoughts and acts might be possible," explains one expert.[7] The Lakota won this one, but they would ultimately lose.

Black Elk himself killed at least three men that day, most memorably (for those who've read *Black Elk Speaks*) scalping two and showing the first of those scalps with pride to his mother. He would unapologetically explain later, with characteristic brevity, "[They] had come to kill our fathers and mothers and us, and it was our country."[8] At one point mid-battle, the young Black Elk also remembered an Oglala beside him falling dead, only to realize a moment later that he was himself still alive. That is how hectic and hellish the scene was. A few moments later, he saw White men's pistols on the ground, fallen from dead hands, and he picked one up. When he scalped that first victim, it was at the urging of the Lakota who had wounded the man. The killer in battle was usually not also the scalper; but then Black Elk shot the wounded man, presumably because scalping a moving man is difficult—especially for a boy.

Forces of Expansion

Only a generation or two before Little Bighorn, Whites and Lakota had often behaved like good neighbors. Sioux leaders helped the explorers Lewis and Clark in their expedition west during the first decade of the century; and during the early years of the Gold Rush in Wyoming and Montana Territories it was the Sioux who, more than any other Native people, seemed friendly and cooperative toward the ever-encroaching caravans of White settlers and explorers.[9]

It is also true that the massacre at Little Bighorn could be described as not in keeping with US government intentions from the decade leading up to it. After the moral failing of Andrew Jackson's Trail of Tears, when Native people of the southeast were forced to relocate west of the Mississippi, resulting in thousands dying, a US congressional commission was appointed to study the problem of Whites in conflict with Natives in the West. That commission concluded in 1867:

> While it cannot be denied that the government of the United States, in the general terms and temper of its legislation, has evinced a desire to deal generously with the Indians, it must be admitted that the actual treatment they have received has been unjust and iniquitous beyond the power of words to express.
>
> Taught by the government that they had rights entitled to respect; when those rights have been assailed by the rapacity of the white man, the arm which should have been raised to protect them has been ever ready to sustain the aggressor.
>
> The history of the Government connections with the Indians is a shameful record of broken treaties and unfulfilled promises.[10]

It amazingly goes on like this for several more paragraphs. It is an early example of commission reports going unread and unheeded.

In 1868, the Fort Laramie Treaty saw the US government and various Indian nations, including the Lakota, agreeing to nonaggression as a way of protecting the mass White migration taking place across Native lands. The treaty even included a commitment to "ensure the civilization" of the Lakota. But the Oglala were nevertheless often fighting with White troops, sometimes beside other tribes, facing White captains and generals with names like Fetterman and Sherman, who have been praised in White history books. Black Elk's father fought in these battles, and his cousin Crazy Horse often starred in them.

This was the case until Ulysses S. Grant, while running for president in 1869, declared his intention to pursue peace with Native people, even admitting some US government moral failure in these matters. He would keep peace in the West, he told the electorate. Red Cloud, who had defeated the army in battle just three years earlier, by 1870 was regarded by many of his own people as nothing more now than a "reservation chief." He traveled to Washington to meet President Grant and said:

> The Great Spirit has seen me naked; and my Great Father [the US government], I have fought against him. . . . The Great Father says he is good and kind to us. I don't think so. . . . The men the Great Father sends to us have no sense—no heart.[11]

But he also began to accept more government assistance, in exchange for nonaggression.

The forces and greed of expansion were too great, overcoming any good intentions that existed. Above all else, White Christians believed that God had given both the grace and responsibility—a "manifest destiny"—to fill the continent with White Christian faith. This notion (but not the phrase)—manifest destiny—can be traced back to the ideas of Thomas Paine, who inspired the American Revolution with his pamphlet, *Common Sense*. It included the lines: "We have it in our power to begin the world over again. A situation, similar to the present, hath not happened since the days of Noah until now."

But it was in 1845 when a doctrine of manifest destiny was named and articulated, in a magazine editorial defending the annexation of Texas into the Union. The people of the United States, it was argued, were designed to fill the land that was given them by God. This was a secularized prophecy built on passages in Scripture beginning with Genesis 1:28, quoted often by Euro-American settlers: "God blessed them, and God said to them, 'Be fruitful and multiply, and fill the earth and subdue it; and have dominion over the fish of the sea and over the birds of the air and over every living thing that moves upon the earth.' " Notice the word in this common English translation: "dominion." That is the sense in which it was taken as a divine directive. The editorial spoke of "our manifest destiny to overspread the continent allotted by Providence for the free development of our yearly multiplying millions."[12] They would indeed expand into every part of the continent, and manifest destiny would be used by political and religious leaders, all of whom were of course Christian in name and White European in background, to describe a divine imperative to conquer what wasn't White and wasn't Christian throughout what eventually became the United States of America.

Gold rushes and land grants added financial incentives, and the first transcontinental railroad, completed when President Grant's term began, provided an efficient means of travel. We forget how transforming was the invention of the railroad. The first direct journey from Paris to Brussels in 1846 was an international event; Alexander Dumas and Victor Hugo were aboard. Suddenly, there was the specter of connecting all of Europe. One Europe could mean an end to war and conflict between nations, many people said then—an ideal that would never materialize. The opposite proved true: railroads made the transportation of weapons and soldiers even easier. That happened on the North American continent as well.

Then, the persistent view of Native Americans as savages seemed to increase the farther one was from Washington, DC. This is how Herman Melville described a typical westerner's view of Native people in his 1857 novel, *The Confidence Man*:

> He hears little from his schoolmasters . . . but histories of
> Indian lying, Indian theft, Indian double-dealing, Indian
> fraud and perfidy, Indian want of confidence, Indian blood-
> thirstiness, Indian diabolism.

Three decades earlier, James Fenimore Cooper's *The Last of the Mohicans* was a bestseller, foretelling the end of Native people as a separate race in America. Cooper had one of his tribal characters say with resignation near the end of the novel, "The pale-faces are masters of the earth, and the time of the red-men has not yet come again."

Different but similarly denigrating terms were used to describe the other more overtly discriminated against minority group—Blacks—millions of whom were kept as slaves at this time. White power was ascendant.

No less influential was Charles Darwin and the powerful new theory of natural selection, first published in 1859 in *On the Origin of Species*. This spread rapidly and rippled beyond the confines of biology. The notion that all that is simple and isolated must ultimately submit to what is complex and intertwined began to feel inevitable and natural, justifying many misuses of power. Whites believed that Natives had to submit to all of this "progress," just like everyone and everything else.

Then Grant began a secret campaign to take the Black Hills, despite making public statements to the contrary. In recent years, historians have uncovered documents that were secret communications between the president and his generals. One is this communiqué from the ranking officer in the West to one of his men in the Black Hills: "At a meeting which occurred in Washington on the 3d of November . . . the President decided that while the orders heretofore issued forbidding the occupation of the Black Hills country by miners should not be rescinded, still no fixed resistance by the military should be made to the miners going in."[13] The level of army troops was increased dramatically as a concerted campaign was set in motion to end interruptions by Natives in White emigration and commerce in the Black Hills and throughout the West. All of this led to what took place at the Battle of Little Bighorn.

CHAPTER THREE

The Great Vision

Something happened to Black Elk the year before the Battle of Little Bighorn that had a more profound effect on his life than any other event or experience.

He was born the son of an Oglala medicine man, who was himself the son of an Oglala medicine man. Grandfather, father, and son each possessed healing powers for their people. It was expected that Black Elk would have visions. Children of all races and backgrounds have dreams that instruct, frighten, or inspire them, but for some children in Native communities, dreams were not only powerful. And dreams did not always take place at night, while sleeping. Dreams and visions were regarded as divine gifts; they were to be heeded.

The role of a vision in his life was not unlike how visions have functioned in the lives of people in every religious tradition who are set apart for special work. And to become a medicine man was to be schooled in counseling, listening, healing, and interpreting. For the Oglala, this entailed a lot of visionary work: in dreams and on what the Oglala regarded "vision quests," a common but pivotal rite of passage. A powerful vision given to such a boy was not just an ordinary dream.

For a Lakota, to seek a vision is akin to prayer, and a Lakota appeal to spirit is similar to a Christian's appeal to the Holy Spirit for inspiration.

Black Elk's "Great Vision," as it came to be called, took place in the summer of 1875 when the Seventh Cavalry was escorting a railroad survey team through the Yellowstone River Valley, one year before the cavalry met Black Elk's people at the Little Bighorn River. Black Elk was only nine years old. The vision came first to him as he sat in a tipi listening to stories after the evening meal. He said that he heard a voice speak to him personally, saying, "It is time."

Then he went outside into the open air, but soon returned to the tipi and fell asleep. It turned out, then, that the Great Vision had not yet really begun. The following day, Black Elk was riding with others on his horse and his legs began to hurt. He was also thirsty, so he dismounted, but then he promptly fell to the ground. His companions had to help him back to his horse and assist in getting him to a tipi to rest. He was apparently suffering from a terrible illness that is unknown to us. This, too, was part of the Great Vision; it was a multiday affair involving his body, mind, and spirit.

Sick with fever and pain in that tipi, his mother worrying over him, he began to see what it was that he was meant to see. He would later recall being carried away on a cloud into the sky. Like John the Baptist in the desert living on locusts or Moses or Jesus fasting for forty days in the desert preparing for a divine encounter, a Lakota would-be spiritual leader would often seek after a vision, denying his body in order to provoke and isolate his soul. Black Elk may have done this, too, but not at the age of nine. This Great Vision was a gift to him. His body was at its weakest, simply because he was near death. Some scholars and other observers have suggested that the sickness he was battling most closely resembles meningitis and that the vision itself is perhaps best described as a near-death experience.[1]

He remembered being carried to a tipi in the sky by two men who wanted to show him his grandfathers. From his sick bed, he remembered getting up:

> Just as I got out of the tipi I could see the two men going back into the clouds and there was a small cloud coming down toward me at the same time, which stood before me. I got on top of the cloud and was raised up, following the two men.[2]

For a Lakota, to go up into the clouds was similar to how a Christian might speak of looking toward heaven. The Lakota word for clouds is the same word that would later be used for heaven; and later in his life Black Elk would understand this similarity and teach it to others: "Matthew 18:3 was one of Black Elk's favorite teachings; it says that unless one becomes like a newborn, one will not enter the kingdom of *mahpiya*," writes Damian Costello.[3]

The Great Vision continues, and the two men show him four groups of horses, representing four directions in which one might go. They prompt him to look to the north, south, east, and west and to observe the earth beneath his feet. Now, in the "Cloud Tipi," he begins to meet his grandfathers. "Your grandfathers all over the world and the earth are having a council and there you are called, so here you are," they tell him.[4]

They hand him water to drink, a bow and arrow, and other tangible gifts including a peace pipe, just one of many sacred Lakota symbols. There are more metaphorical gifts that they give him, as well, such as a "flowering stick," which seems to be like a tree placed at the center of the world, almost a vision of a new Eden. Black Elk says:

> They put the sacred stick into the center of the hoop and you could hear birds singing all kinds of songs by this flowering stick and the people and animals all rejoiced and hollered.[5]

They gift him with wisdom and self-awareness, telling him not to be afraid, that he is destined to become powerful in the ways of healing and that it is up to him to lead his people down the red road toward the sacred hoop, to become a great nation, even though his people will soon have great troubles. An analogy to Moses ascending the mountain alone to hear from God in the clouds that he is called to lead the people Israel out of bondage in Egypt is inescapable.

That "red road" could have first been understood as referring to Lakota skin color, or to the Native path generally, but it would later be revealed to Black Elk, after his conversion to Catholicism, as symbolizing the way of Jesus. He would use a visual catechism in his teaching that showed the path of salvation history moving through Hebrew Scripture using the color black, and then the coming of Christ, when the road becomes red.

Together, Black Elk and the sixth grandfather travel in the clouds to the world's highest mountains—namely, Harney Peak, at more than seventy-two hundred feet—from which they can see everything taking place: the famine of their people, the buffalo herds vanishing, riverbeds drying up, and there Black Elk is given more sacred gifts—herbs, a mysterious spear, and additional healing powers to cure his people and their broken world.

He came away from this experience believing himself to be divinely inspired and sanctioned—indeed, even commanded—to save his people and the planet. This healer came away from this profound religious experience identifying with the spiritual powers of his tradition, emboldened to fight hunger, sickness, and disharmony.

Still, the Great Vision was not over. The grandfathers had to take him back home, back to that tipi where he lay sick and dying with fever. An eagle showed them the way to that place, and it seemed that everyone looking at that sick child was still there, worried and sad. Black Elk's mother was panic-stricken. She would later tell him that he had been gone (medically speaking, likely, in a coma) for twelve days.

Then the Great Vision was over. Black Elk was charged with spiritual authority at a young age. He had become the "sixth grandfather," with the responsibility to build upon the work of the previous five, who showed him the world in its past, present, and future. "By becoming the sixth grandfather through the vision experience, Black Elk was identified as the spirit of all mankind. And the vision foreshadowed his life as a holy man—as thinker, healer, teacher," explains Raymond DeMallie.[6]

Essential for the direction of the rest of his life and pivotal for understanding the scope and meaning of it, of his Great Vision Black Elk later told Neihardt: "I saw that the sacred hoop of my people was one of many hoops that made one circle." The Oglala were not meant to be superior, nor were they intended to live in isolation. Black Elk came away called to heal more than just his own people; the sacred hoop was a symbol that stood for all people everywhere. This same broader understanding of the sacred—and his own calling—would allow him, later, to see another religious tradition and how it might make sense of himself and his place in the world.

What Did It Mean?

So much has been made of Black Elk's Great Vision that it is worth pausing to consider it from revelatory, textual, and artistic perspectives. The Lakota were prepared to receive it as a divine revelation. So, too, were many of the people who read *Black Elk Speaks* with a kind of post-Christian enthusiasm.

Textually, it is interesting to contemplate how, as well as when, the Great Vision came into existence, outside of Black Elk's personal experience. It seems to be generally agreed that he was not yet considered a man in Oglala society both before and after his Great Vision. It took time for his position among his people to still be made clear, despite what he had seen and heard. This is true of prophets in every community, in every religious tradition. It is also unclear just how much Black Elk shared the vision with others while he was a boy and when he was a teenager. He became a broodier boy, remaining silent much of the time, even as he remembered those tools with which he would bring healing to his people and the hope that would live on in him despite the foreboding.

The Great Vision truly became a phenomenon when John Neihardt prompted it out of Black Elk more than half a century later. To consider it artistically is another way to say, consider the personality of the one who received it. Black Elk was born to be a mystic and trained to be a medicine man. Joseph Epes Brown, who interviewed him in 1947, only three years before he died, said: "This responsibility to 'bring to life the flowering tree of his people' haunted Black Elk all his life and caused him much suffering. Although he had been given the power to heal his people in the ways of his grandfathers, he did not understand by what means the vision could be fulfilled."[7]

Is it likely that a less sensitive, less perceptive, less artistic boy would have seen and heard it? "Both the Lakota and Christian religions maintain that there is continual contact with the spirit world, at least in a materially supportive way, even though ordinary people are little conscious of it," explains an expert in both traditions.[8] This is perhaps how all personal communications with the divine take place, if they do at all: only through people who are prepared to receive them, and Black Elk was.

CHAPTER FOUR

Indian on Show

"Civilization is a huge and insatiable beast. It feeds on everything."

—Eric Vuillard[1]

What happened next to Black Elk, after the Great Vision, we have already seen in the travails of the Battle of Little Bighorn, the fight for survival on the Plains of his people, the hope before the pain and dissolution after Greasy Grass. He was a young man who had to figure out his place in the world and, like the rest of his people, how he would survive.

The next character in his story is a White man who was already famous by the time Custer fell dead. A scout in the army serving in the Western territories, William "Buffalo Bill" Cody earned his nickname in a contest killing bison on the Great Plains, then used it to set himself apart. Like Custer, Cody was a publicity hound. His most famous stunt of all took place in days immediately following Custer's death when he not only shot and killed a Cheyenne—one of a few hundred who were attempting to cross northwestern Nebraska to join Sitting Bull and Crazy Horse near Little Bighorn—but scalped him, holding up the scalp to show the warrior's friends while Cody's fellow soldiers surrounded and protected him. This took place on July 17, 1876, at Warbonnet Creek and is known as "The First Scalp for Custer" because Cody told newspaper reporters that's what he yelled at the Cheyenne. Three months later and Cody was playing the part of Wild Bill on stage, reenacting his own scene—something he'd do again and again for decades, often using the phrase "The Red Right Hand" to describe his braggadocio.

Even before Warbonnet Creek, Cody was known to an adventure-hungry American public through magazine stories such as "Buffalo Bill, King of the Border Men," which began to be serialized in *Street and Smith's New York Weekly* in 1869. Encouraged by Cody, writers romanticized his life and the dangers and exploits involved in "settling the West." By 1872, he was starring in his first stage production in Chicago, playing Wild Bill. Critics panned him, but crowds loved him, and his good looks were often mentioned. Like Custer, he had curly locks that people associated with a suave, courageous, man of the West.

Wild Bill left the army soon after making his scalping incident famous, to create a full-time career of his showmanship. He founded Buffalo Bill's Wild West in 1883, hiring cowboys and Native people to travel in a large company, circus-style, from town to town, and eventually abroad, performing scenes from the "Wild West" that was already full of legends in the imagination of Americans.

Indians were fascinating, particularly and especially as they were vanishing. As a French writer has recently put it:

> Spectacle is the origin of the world. Tragedy stands before us, motionless and strangely anachronistic. And so, in Chi-

cago, at the World's Columbian Exposition of 1893 commemorating the 400th anniversary of Columbus's voyage, a display of relics on a stall in the central aisle included the desiccated corpse of a newborn Indian baby. There were twenty-one million visitors.[2]

Cody understood how a combination of spontaneity, danger, and the unusual—a precursor to reality TV—would draw large audiences. He understood the intrigue and drama of historical characters that had already become myth-like in America, such as Daniel Boone and Billy the Kid. In addition to characters (real and imagined) from the American West, Cody added others to his shows that in the xenophobic fashion of the time were described as "Turks," "Arabs," "gauchos," and "Mongols." Other actors were hired precisely because they, too, had name recognition. For instance, in some of the first film ever shot, inventor Thomas Edison captured bits of Cody's Wild West showing young Annie Oakley with her rifle hitting targets, cowboys waving hats in the air while riding bucking broncos, Indians on parade in colorful outfits, and Native men performing a Ghost Dance, then a buffalo dance.

Cody's show had real Indians as its centerpiece. He did not originate this performance form. There were earlier traveling troupes of Native people from North America, most notably Inuit from Labrador and Nuxalk from British Columbia, who were induced by a Norwegian explorer in 1880 and 1885 to go to Europe to perform their dances and rituals to large crowds.[3] People came to gasp and point, to see them reenact the very moments of terror that saw those same Indians losing hegemony; they were probably also seeking that lost "noble savage," uncorrupted by civilization, whom they'd read about in Romantic literature.

With his (in)famous show, Cody was "glorifying conquest."[4]

In November 1886, Black Elk did something that his in-terpreters will always have difficulty explaining: he left behind the Great Plains and most of his fellow Oglala to join the traveling troupe of Buffalo Bill Cody on the road. He wasn't alone in this. The great Lakota chief, Sitting Bull, for instance, had preceded him a year earlier. But why would they do it?

Black Elk spent two years touring the United States and Europe, playing the part of an American Indian for cheering crowds. Like P. T. Barnum before him, Cody understood that success of a traveling variety show depended, in part, on domesticating the unusual, violent, and frightening, in a controlled environment. For Barnum, it was wild animals; for Cody's Wild West Show, it was Native people, about which most Whites knew only what they'd seen screaming in the headlines of newspapers.

One imagines that, for the Native American performers, the feeling of reenacting "Custer's Last Stand" was com-pletely different than it was for the crowd who watched them. Perhaps this explanation is the best to grasp what Black Elk and the other Native people were feeling:

> It was almost as if Buffalo Bill's lurid re-creation of the West—in his rendition, at least, the Indians got to defeat Custer over and over again—possessed more authenticity than the wretchedness of [life on the reservation].[5]

The troupe traveled by train, on Black Elk's first outing, through the outpost cities of Omaha and St. Louis, across the Ohio River Valley, east to Manhattan's Madison Square Garden, where they played for three straight months. The show opened on November 24 and didn't close until Febru-ary 22.[6] It included Indians stalking and fighting each other, elk and buffalo "roaming" the stage, loud Winchester rifles firing, cowboys wrangling, and stagecoach robberies in process. Black Elk was glad to earn some real money, but he also surely knew he was being exploited. There was even a sexual element of the show to the White paying customers, many of them leering at the unusual and scantily clad with pleasure. One local newspaper reporter made mention in his Thanksgiving Day review of "the fair sex" looking "with interest upon the dancers," who included "almost entirely nude braves, with their hides tinted according to the latest thing in war paint."[7]

Turning point battles against Indigenous Americans were known well enough in the big cities in the East, from popular newspaper reports and even reenactments on theatrical stages, such that when the troupe played Custer's Last Stand, and Cody, playing the part of Lt. Colonel Custer, emerged from the fighting victorious, everyone understood that this was a fantasy and cheered thunderously. At the same time, they were truth-telling of what White people expected for the future.

After the long run at Madison Square Garden, many of the Lakota (there were about one hundred in all) went home to Pine Ridge Reservation, but not Black Elk. He stayed with the troupe for their trip across the Atlantic.

For Queen and Continent

In *The Adventures of Buffalo Bill*, his autobiography, Cody wrote this about his Wild West Show:

> The reason for its enormous popularity and increase is that it is almost unique among shows and plays of every kind. For it gives to the audience a real picture, with real characters, a most exciting period of civilization in this country that never has existed anywhere else, and that never will exist here again.[8]

He wasn't wrong.

After a two-week North Atlantic sea journey, during which Black Elk was terribly nauseated, they landed in London, the most populated city on earth. It was April 1887. Black Elk was still only twenty years old.

One of the most enticing features of Cody's show, on the road and abroad, was not what happened under the tent but in the encampment outside. This is where the showman arranged for a re-creation of Native American camp life. One London newspaper described the expected scene at Earl's Court in a story two days before the troupe's ship landed in England: "In the center of the vast arena—which already reminds one of the interior of the Colosseum—are placed rocks and fir trees, backed by a panorama of Rocky Mountain scenery 500 foot long. Here Buffalo Bill (the Hon. J. Cody) and 200 Indians, cowboys, and scouts will illustrate the wild sports of the Far West, assisted by no less than 250 animals, including many buffalos."[9] It was probably copy written by Cody himself, always his best publicist. Some of those expected buffalo were in fact lost at sea and had to be thrown overboard, something which Black Elk likely witnessed in horror.

While in England, they performed for Queen Victoria— whom Black Elk referred to as "Grandmother England"—not once but twice, the second command performance being held at Windsor Castle. We know that Black Elk danced specifically for the Queen. He must have hoped that she would understand him or would at least come to appreciate something of the ways of his fallen people. He probably did not realize that she was sovereign over an empire that subjected and colonized Native people on other continents, just as Euro-Americans were doing to the Oglala in North America.

Wild West ran in London for six months with an average daily attendance of at least thirty thousand.[10] The newspapers ran stories daily about the show and detailed Indian sightings around town. One of Black Elk's fellow Native performers, Red Shirt, featured prominently in some of these, including one account of him being received in the royal box at a theatre production. Then they moved on to Birmingham, the second-largest city in England, where one night Black Elk was arrested for public drunkenness in a pub. Then they went to Manchester, where the tour ended to more acclaim at the end of April 1888.

Together with a few other Native performers, Black Elk missed the train from Manchester to Kingston upon Hull in northeastern England on the North Sea, where a ship was going to take everyone south along the coast of England through the straits of Dover and back into the North Atlantic toward New York City. With the help of one of their company who spoke English, the group then made their way by train to London, where they soon joined a smaller, rival troupe (called "Mexican Joe's") that was in England performing "Indian shows." Not sure what else to do, they spent the spring, summer, and early fall doing more shows. They then joined the troupe headed to Paris—where Black Elk briefly had a White girlfriend—and then went on to Brussels and Naples, and back again to England. Finally, Black Elk narrowly escaped a devastating fire in an arena in Manchester in February 1889.

Almost a year after missing the train to Hull, he was ready to make his way home. He was homesick and had earned enough money to buy his passage. Mexican Joe's headed back to Paris for more shows, and Black Elk joined them, but then was either sick or injured and unable to perform. He was hurt in the Manchester fire, but he also seems to have fallen from his mustang during a performance. He told Neihardt that in Paris he again saw his French girlfriend and her family, who were kind to him. Biographer Joe Jackson argues that the Paris sojourn was entirely for the purposes of seeing again the French girlfriend that he had left behind and that perhaps she was pregnant with their child, but that's speculation. Black Elk finally sailed from Paris back to the United States, and soon enough he was back in the Black Hills again.

We may perhaps glean from *Black Elk Speaks* the ultimate reason for Black Elk leaving home, despite his family's pleading with him not to, to join Bill Cody's Wild West. Desiring to fulfill what the grandfathers had seen for his future and his life's purpose, to bring healing and wholeness to his people, Black Elk seems to have believed that joining the big show and leaving home for strange lands was a good idea "because I might learn some secret . . . that would help my people somehow. . . . Maybe if I could see the great world of the Wasichu, I could understand how to bring the sacred hoop together and make the tree bloom again at the center of it."[11] He used *wasichu* to mean people of White, European descent. In Lakota it literally means, "greedy person who takes the fat." This is the only reason that seems to make sense of it.

CHAPTER FIVE

The Slaughter at Wounded Knee

A great deal has happened in Black Elk's life since the Battle of Little Bighorn. He has crossed the Atlantic twice on a steamer, danced for a queen, performed throughout Europe, survived a fire, made a girlfriend, seen too much death and disease, and established his practice as a Lakota medicine man.

Now, we see how he was formed by the events of one fateful day—the second of those two sets of dates that chapter 2 began by saying were essential for understanding the Lakota experience and Black Elk's life. He was twenty-four years old.

Looking back, remembering the painful years between that brief feeling of victory at the Battle of Little Bighorn and what happened on December 29, 1890, the slaughter of his people at Wounded Knee, Black Elk would say: "[O]nly crazy or very foolish men would sell their Mother Earth," followed by, "Sometimes I think it might have been better if we had stayed together and made them kill us all."[1]

The Dawes Act of 1887 had introduced and forced private ownership of land upon Indigenous people, subdividing large swaths of Native land into allotments for heads of families. This was supposed to lead the Oglala to plowing as White farmers do, building log houses, wearing Western clothes, visiting cities, and leaning toward Western ideas of progress. There were some Native people who had already assimilated in these ways, many more who refused to do so, and those who looked with scorn on those who had.

Between passage of the Dawes Act and Wounded Knee, a new religious ritual was imagined in Native communities desperate to be rid of White encroachment and yearning for their old ways of life free of White entanglements. This ritual was also a belief system. It began in the Nevada territory among the Paiute in 1899. The Ghost Dance—sometimes called a messianic movement or, in the case of the Lakota expression, more of a millenarian movement that looked to a transformed "end of days" time of cataclysm and trans-formation—was born. It was in some respects just a dance, but in other ways, it was much more. Ghost Dancers often wore special outer garments that they believed would keep them safe from bullets. They talked of how the world to come would be free of White people and the problems they brought, including disease. A more sophisticated way to put this is recently summarized by the brilliant Native writer, Nick Estes: "imagining and enacting an anticolonial Indig-enous future free from the death world brought on by settler invasion."[2] The Ghost Dance took on a fervency of practice and created enthusiastic believers—believing in the power of Native people to determine their own destiny with help from the Great Spirit. It frightened White people looking on, who wanted to keep the tribes in their designated places. The great Sitting Bull was one of its prominent defenders, and he would soon be killed because of it.

The death of Custer continued to reverberate throughout the states and territories after Little Bighorn. The general's reputation in death had become almost messianic:

> Custer was elevated into an exemplary Christian knight, and the hill of his Last Stand became "a Golgotha" of America's "frontier settlements."[3]

Response was swift and then frequent from politicians and in public opinion: the "Indian problem" had to be solved once and for all. Add to it the Ghost Dance, which reached the Indian Office in Washington, DC, in the spring of 1890, six months before Wounded Knee, and the time was ripe for more deadly conflict.[4]

Oglala leaders were wandering, unsure where to go, where to be safe, what to do next. There were other, smaller, battles and skirmishes. Black Elk took part in some of these. At Fort Robinson in Nebraska, his cousin Crazy Horse was killed on September 5, 1877, in a struggle as US forces attempted to arrest him. Many Oglala, then, including Black Elk, traveled to Canada to be near Sitting Bull, who also had fought bravely at Little Bighorn but then made his way to Canada. The US Army could not pursue them there. But beyond that measure of safety, their existence, especially during the winters, was difficult, and they were surrounded by many old tribal enemies who had little reason to be kind or generous with resources.

Still just a teenager, Black Elk continued to feel that *Wakan Tanka* and the grandfathers had laid upon him a great responsibility. Remembering that time, he said, "I recalled my vision now and then and wondered when my duty was to come."[5] They remained in Canada until early in 1880, and then made their way back to the Black Hills.

Newspaper editorials and elected officials called for brutal severity, as one might declare war on a foreign enemy. There were more forced removals to reservation land, as the federal government continued to enforce the Dawes Act, telling Natives they had to learn European-style agriculture and how to stay put, creating European-style villages and occupations. In the years leading up to Wounded Knee, there was no Native life to go back to that would have made sense to the Oglala and other tribes.

President Benjamin Harrison, who assumed the office in March the year before Wounded Knee, sent more troops to the region. "[N]early one-third of the entire U.S. Army descended on the Lakota country in mid-November. It was an invasion."[6]

Then came December. Crazy Horse had already been dead for thirteen years. He died a hero, convinced by the US military to give himself up: "[H]e did so because he had obtained a promise from the army that his people could continue to roam the sacred Black Hills as they always had. . . . When he discovered that the promises were all a ruse, he rose up for all to see and fought to be free once again, and was killed doing so. Today Crazy Horse stands as a man who sacrificed himself to maintain the Lakota way of life."[7] Sitting Bull was away.

Black Elk was in the Pine Ridge Reservation, and it was four days after Christmas. He was twenty-four.

This defining confrontation took place between US soldiers and members of the Lakota, Northern Cheyenne, and Arapaho tribes across Wounded Knee Creek at Pine Ridge. Black Elk heard the big Hotchkiss guns firing from miles away and quickly prepared himself with red face paint and sacred stick, mounting one of the fastest horses in his care and riding into the fray. He no longer felt comfortable with killing, so he carried no weapons. He was also no longer the boy who sought manhood through scalping at Little Bighorn. Black Elk was now a holy man.

But by the time he arrived, the massacre (it was no battle) was in its late stages. The initial killing was done; now the soldiers were hunting remaining men, women, and even children. His Lakota brothers and sisters were trapped in a ravine and still being fired upon by the cavalry. When Black Elk saw this, he and others who were rushing to the scene responded instinctually. They hurried in to save who they could. Then they rushed the cavalry itself, almost fanatically, in the way that Black Elk's cousin Crazy Horse once did. "He charged at the soldiers," writes one biographer, "armed only with his sacred bow. He held it before him as they aimed. Bullets snapped around him, but none found their mark. He rode within twenty yards of the line and some of the soldiers jumped up and ran. He shouted his defiance in their faces."[8]

The massacre went on for hours. Many press accounts made it seem that what happened was a "heat of the moment" confrontation that went bad, but that wasn't true. As the Center for American Indian Research and Native Studies has concluded:

> Based on the evidence, the soldiers probably spent the day hunting down and killing Lakotas until around sunset. The horrific slaughter at Wounded Knee was not an "unfortunate incident" or a "battle." The disarming of women and men, the indiscriminate killing of children, women, and men, and then the hunting down and killing of more innocent children, women, and men was horrific.[9]

Black Elk would lament the tragedy the rest of his life. There are many quotations from him from interviews, mostly those conducted with Neihardt, and later with Joseph Epes Brown (in 1947), that reveal a sad pessimism and a sense of resignation. The massacre of his people and loss of their ways of life are the main context for understanding this. When looking back over the course of his long life, it was difficult not to see, above all else, loss. The reported last words of his cousin Crazy Horse, as he lay dying, reveal this same spirit: "We preferred our own way of living. . . . All we wanted was peace and to be left alone. . . . I came here . . . to talk . . . but was not given a chance. They tried to confine me, I tried to escape, and a soldier ran his bayonet into me. I have spoken."[10]

Black Elk remembered later how he felt, admitting: "I wanted a chance to kill soldiers." Until he died, Black Elk would wonder if he should have or could have done more to protect his people that day. Convinced by the great Sioux warrior-turned-statesman, Red Cloud, to stop fighting for the sake of the women and children, Black Elk and others had acquiesced and made their way to Pine Ridge looking only for peace. They found the opposite. Black Elk later said: "They stood in two lines with their guns held in front of them as we went through. . . . And so it was all over."[11]

However, as always, the Black Elk recorded by Neihardt told less than half of the story. As others would discover, when more fully researching the life, Black Elk was also sad and melancholy because of a lack of hope among his people and the rising secularism that he was witnessing in their changing ways. Children were often away at boarding schools, learning nothing of Lakota ways. Men were often farming, which rarely suited them, or trying to pursue other Euro-American ways of making a living. The buffalo were gone. The loss of Indian life and culture was massive. It wasn't Christianity per se that was to blame. In fact, Christian inspiration and teaching would become Black Elk's chosen antidote— and with great success.[12]

The Medal of Honor was bestowed on dozens of US troops for bravery at Wounded Knee, which, needless to say, does not come close to describing how Lakota historians describe the actions of the Seventh Cavalry on that day. And to visit the solemn place where this killing took place, today, in the middle of Pine Ridge Reservation, is to witness what has happened to the Oglala over the last century-plus. There is no monument or visitor's center, and the graves are poor.

This often-quoted passage from the final page of *Black Elk Speaks* has Black Elk looking back and remembering what happened:

> I did not know then how much was ended. When I look back now from this high hill of my old age, I can still see the butchered women and children lying heaped and scattered all along the crooked gulch as plain as when I saw them with eyes still young. And I can see that something else died there in the bloody mud, and was buried in the blizzard. A people's dream died there. It was a beautiful dream.[13]

That day ended any optimism one might have held for the future of the Lakota on what was once their land. US forces had set out that day to disarm them—to take away their weapons—and when one resisted, members of the Seventh Cavalry began firing upon what were by then unarmed men. But it was also much more than that. The build-up and animosity were extreme, and the soldiers were filled with hate. The cavalry massacred at least 150 Lakota men, women, and children and left more than fifty others injured. One of the three reporters at the scene, Charles Arnet of *The New York Herald* newspaper, watched the frenzy of the killing and it made him ill. He sat down, later writing: "I drew out my old pipe—a never-failing friend in such emergencies—and concluded that those boys of the Seventh Cavalry were too excited to think of anything but vengeance."[14]

PART TWO

CATECHIST

CHAPTER SIX

Missionaries and Priests

Three days after the Massacre at Wounded Knee, a Santee Dakota man, born in Minnesota, fresh from Dartmouth College and medical school in Boston, where he graduated in 1887 and 1889, arrived at the scene. A blizzard had passed through the Black Hills the day after the massacre, and the day before Dr. Charles Eastman's arrival to survey and help the survivors at Pine Ridge Reservation. He recorded his thoughts from that morning:

> It took all of my nerve to keep my composure in the face of this spectacle, and of the excitement and grief of my Indian companions, nearly every one of whom was crying aloud or singing his death song. . . . Although they had been lying untended in the snow and cold for two days and nights, a number had survived.

Then Eastman, who was born named Hakadah, meaning "pitiful last" in Lakota, because his Lakota mother died in childbirth, added: "All this was a severe ordeal for one who had so lately put all his faith in the Christian love and lofty ideals of the white man."[1]

* * *

What took place in the four hundred years between Christopher Columbus reaching the New World and Black Elk's generation has been accurately called a "European invasion." It had disastrous results for the Native population.[2] Some of the disaster was intentional, in the form of land grabbing and forced exile, and some was unintentional, in the form of diseases the Europeans brought with them, which killed more Native Americans than did European guns.

Columbus, like most Europeans who followed him, viewed all Indigenous people as either potential converts or potential slaves. On that first famous voyage in 1492, he wrote: "I have not found the human monsters which many people expected. On the contrary, the whole population is very well made. They are not Negroes as in Guinea, and their hair is straight . . . but they are strong nonetheless." He believes he's describing a different species from his own. Then he describes Natives as defenseless ("They have no iron. Their spears are made of cane."); ignorant of Western ways ("[W]hen I showed them swords, they took them by the edge and cut themselves out of ignorance."); useful ("They should be good servants . . . for I have observed that they soon repeat anything that is said to them."); and credulous ("I believe that they would easily be made Christians.").[3]

This was the way of the Western mind, with few exceptions. It was widely believed that, unless a people were Christian, they were unfit to inhabit the New World. This way of thinking was sanctioned at the highest levels of religion. Pope Nicholas V promulgated a papal bull (*Dum Diversas*, "Until Different") in 1452 declaring that the slave trade was legitimate. The holy pontiff's intention then was to allow the Portuguese king to conquer lands dominated by "Saracens" (what Christians called Arab Muslims) and take them as slaves if necessary. So-called pagans were also to be freely handled this way. Pope Alexander VI confirmed this judgment in 1493 in relation to exploration of the Americas and elsewhere, praising the notion of "Christian Empire," saying that the sovereign of Spain was responsible to propagate it. A few decades later, in 1537, a papal bull of Paul III called *Sublimis Deus*, "The Sublime God," showed small progress by declaring Native peoples fully human, even though heathen, and thus forbidding Catholic nations from enslaving them.

For the mostly Protestants who came from Europe to settle what became the United States, these notions were also understood, as was the idea of manifest destiny as an expression of Christ's Great Commission. An anthropologist explains it this way:

> When white men first witnessed Indians impersonating animal spirits in costume and dance, and worshiping rocks and rainbows, they failed to see this as a form of deep religious expression. To their Christian minds, these were deplorable pagan rites. Worship of more than one deity, and sacrificial offerings directed at the natural world, stamped Indians as a misguided, lesser form of mankind. Here were Christless heathens crying to be rescued from eternal damnation.
>
> For their part most Native Americans were not averse initially to Christianity. Before the white man appeared, tribes had absorbed new waves of religious thought. To them a fresh form of worship did not negate the old. The great value they placed on their own traditional beliefs made them especially curious about the magical deeds of this new medicine man, the Son of God.[4]

But as Luther Standing Bear, a Lakota writer and leader of Black Elk's generation, said: "We did not think of the great open plains, the beautiful rolling hills, the winding streams with tangled growth, as *wild*. Only to the white man was nature a *wilderness* and only to him was it *infested* with *wild* animals and *savage* people. To us it was tame. Earth was bountiful and we were surrounded with the blessings of the Great Mystery."[5]

Three Centuries of Missions

With those early explorers came priests and missionaries. French priests came from New France (Canada), south. Spanish priests came from New Spain (Mexico), north. The *Requerimeinto*, or Spanish "Requirement" of 1513, was a declaration by the monarchy that any Native people on land taken into possession by Spanish explorers should be given a choice between slavery and salvation. With a solemnity that mocked what is truly solemn, this document was often read aloud—in Castilian—to Native people who gathered to see what the explorers and settlers were all about.

Spanish Franciscans established missions throughout Florida in the 1570s, followed by New Mexico a decade later. Wherever a mission was planted, there were farms and military installations, too. Natives were expected to convert and join in Christian life. The French took a slightly lighter approach, moving in smaller numbers, often integrating themselves into Native tribes and communities. Protestant missionaries were doing likewise in New England and Virginia, but it would be a century before they would move further west, and then they did not have the backing of a foreign nation and its military. So in 1819, the US Congress appropriated $10,000 (about $250,000 in today's money) to pay missionaries willing to live among Native American tribes and convert them to Christianity, in the hope that this would make Native people more congenial to US westward expansion. Conversion to Christianity was supposed to entail adopting Western styles of dress and building houses. Assimilation was government doctrine, as missionaries made their way to the Great Plains.

Most missionaries knew nothing but their own standards of culture, literacy, decorum, and religion. For example, Rev. Stephen Return Riggs, a Protestant among the Dakota Sioux in Minnesota territory at the time of Little Bighorn, taught would-be missionaries that the "gospel of soap was a necessary adjunct and outgrowth of the Gospel of Salvation."[6] Most had little interest in understanding Native ways before they set out to conform them to European ones.

There are examples of early missionaries who defended the rights of Native people. Bartolomé de las Casas, the Spanish Dominican, for instance, rebuked his countrymen for violent acts committed against Indians, but he also advocated removing them from their homes to enculturate them with European values. Certain passages of Scripture assisted in this work, such as, "[I]f anyone is in Christ, there is a new creation: everything old has passed away; see, everything has become new!" (2 Cor 5:17). This was made to mean that Indigenous ways of life were to be abandoned for Christ. Three centuries later, during Black Elk's lifetime, the first Episcopal bishop of Minnesota, Rev. Henry Benjamin Whipple, was often genuinely committed to serving the Dakota and Ojibwe, but he did so most of all by building Indian missions to educate them like Whites.[7] And the phrase "off the reservation" became an idiom to deride those who are supposed to stay put and do what they are told but dare to attempt otherwise.

Early encounters between missionaries and Natives were rarely recorded. One account appears in the diaries left behind by a French American fur trader who was active along the Upper Missouri River between the 1830s and early 1870s:

> All Indians believe in a Great Spirit, the ruler of all they see and know. . . . In conversation with them I found much pleasure in hearing their stories, which they relate with great eloquence, using a great many figurative expressions. I had some books printed in their language, which I brought with me from St. Paul. These were religious books, gotten up by missionaries of Minnesota, containing Noah's Ark, Jonah swallowed by the whale, and other miracles; at which they would laugh heartily when I read to them, and then say, "Do the whites believe all this rubbish, or are they stories such as we make up to amuse ourselves on long winter nights?" They were very fond of having me read them such stories; that big boat tickled them, and how could Noah get all those animals into it was the question. Then they would say, "The white man can beat us in making up stories."[8]

The Jesuits came from New France and Belgium. They first arrived on the continent in 1609. Within sixty years, they were approaching the Great Plains, establishing a mission in Green Bay, Wisconsin, and thirty years later, one in Illinois territory. When they were suppressed as a religious order in France in the 1760s, they were expelled from the Louisiana territory. Pope Pius VII, however, restored them to good standing in 1814, and within fifteen years, Jesuits were back establishing missions in the Plains among the Sioux. In fact, it is when the Jesuits came to live among the Oglala that their priests became known as *Sina Sapa*, "black robes," for their distinctive outerwear.

At this point, the figure of Red Cloud, one of the most important Oglala leaders from the generation that struggled with President Grant and fought with Custer, reenters our story. Red Cloud was four decades and two decades older than Black Elk and Crazy Horse. Red Cloud didn't participate in the Battle of the Greasy Grass. Instead, a year earlier, he led a Native delegation to Washington, DC, to meet with the president, his secretary of the Interior, and minister of Indian Affairs, seeking to convince the government to cease explorations of Indian lands and stem the tide of the gold rush. A treaty was written that offered money to the tribes and a negotiated resettlement. Red Cloud refused to sign it. He did, however, invite the Jesuits to start a school to educate Oglala children.

Black robes were perceived as having more in common with the Oglala than their Protestant counterparts—not because Episcopal missionaries wore white robes instead of black ones but because the ritual and practices of Catholicism seemed closer to those of Native medicine men. Many of the Jesuit priests who served at Pine Ridge Reservation, starting with the teachers invited by Red Cloud, to the Oglala resembled a *wicasa wakan*, or "holy man." Jesuits have been living and ministering in Pine Ridge Reservation ever since Red Cloud invited them to start that first school. It was also Jesuits who helped complete the first Bible translation into Lakota, in 1885, picking up on work begun several decades earlier by French fur traders.[9]

Natives Becoming Christians

It is into this troubled context that Black Elk became Nicholas Black Elk upon being baptized and confirmed in the Roman Catholic Church on December 6, 1904.

What complicates his conversion is not only his indelible record over the next four decades as an exemplary catechist and evangelist—a missionary in his own right—but a comment he purportedly made to his friend John Neihardt when Neihardt asked what was the motivating factor for him to join a White church. With all the beauty and spiritual meaning already surrounding him and his work as an Oglala holy man, why did he need the White man's religion? Black Elk is recorded as replying, "Because my children have to live in this world."

"I could never forget those words," Neihardt's daughter later wrote, when she recounted the episode. She was with her father that day in Black Elk's home:

> Previously we had been told about something that happened when he was young and just beginning to use his powers to cure illness. The youthful medicine man was praying for the sick person's recovery and using his rattle as part of a healing ceremony when a priest burst into the tepee, grabbed young Black Elk and pulled him rudely outside. Then he took Black Elk's sacred rattle, threw it to the ground, and stamped on it, admonishing the surprised young man that he should never use such "heathen" objects again.[10]

Hilda Neihardt adds: "I have wondered what real difference there could possibly be between a Sioux holy man's shaking his rattle up and down and a priest's swinging his golden censer back and forth." She then explains that her father pushed the matter no further and felt no need to explain himself. But with what we know now about the depths of Black Elk's faith, it is clear that Neihardt missed a great deal.

Also now, with Nicholas Black Elk being considered for canonization, many who learn about his life might question the idea of honoring a man known to have been one of the Oglala who killed US soldiers at the Battle of Little Bighorn, where Custer died. It isn't as if Black Elk repudiated his actions at Little Bighorn later in life, after his conversion. Still, one might argue, why *would* or *should* he repudiate them? He was defending himself and his people against overpowering aggressors.

Yet another perspective, because of Neihardt's powerful mythmaking, as well as the complicated witness of the subject himself, is to see Black Elk as a unique mystical visionary, without ties to any religious tradition, let alone the "White man's" religion. There are some scholars of Native American religion who conclude: "The essential religiousness of the man has transcended the problems of translation and cross-cultural communication."[11]

I think the truth is found in none of these three but in this: He was both a genuine Oglala and a faithful Catholic. When he became Catholic, he decided it was his duty to love and serve his enemies, as Christ taught, and this had an impact on his Oglala worldview. But he still maintained his Native identity. He was able to hold two religious identities together, and his doing so was one of the sources of his profound witness for the Catholic faith among his people.

CHAPTER SEVEN

From Oglala to Rome

It is usually assumed—in our popular culture and class-rooms—that Christianity has been nothing but an upsetting force to Native American ritual, religion, and life since missionaries first introduced Christianity to Indigenous people. Our understanding of once-iconic figures and moments like Christopher Columbus and the first Thanksgiving have been forever changed as we've been sensitized to historical realities of what happened to the first nations. The colonialism of Christianity has become the normative explanation for how Christianity has functioned in the life of the Oglala and every other tribe of Native people.

The American Indian Movement (AIM) had this as one of their primary talking points when the movement began in the 1960s. It became common to say what since then has become a staple of nearly every high school textbook: "The missionaries came with the Bible in one hand and the sword in the other. They had the book and we had the land. Now we've got the book—and they've got the land."[1] One of those activists, Russell Means, an Oglala actor (*The Last of the Mohicans*, *Natural Born Killers*), said in an interview before his death in 2012:

We are yet to be considered human beings, even though the Pope issued a papal bull in 1898 that declared us to be human beings. But to show you the institutional racism, the sports teams are still using the Indians as mascots. The mainstream churches still have missionaries on Indian reservations at the beginning of the new millennium. They've had us captured on reservations a minimum of 125 years, and yet they still have missionaries here.[2]

But we have such a hard time seeing Nicholas Black Elk for who he was if we cannot see beyond the mold of this common understanding.

The Spark for His Conversion

In the winter of 1886, when Black Elk signed on with showman Bill Cody's traveling performers, he also agreed to be baptized into the Episcopal Church. It was a required formality, and apparently, Black Elk thought nothing of it.[3]

Nearly two decades later, on December 6, 1904, he was baptized into the Roman Catholic Church at the age of thirty-eight. Perhaps Black Elk failed to mention his previous baptism, because if he had, it would probably have been respected by the Jesuits; or perhaps that previous event had made no impact on him. In any case, the story of how this happened is the story of all that's in this book, and the part, in microcosm, about where and when the ultimate prodding toward conversion took place is in and of itself fascinating. It took place over a period of two or three weeks.

It was probably mid-November 1904 when it first began. The setting is a tent in which a boy lay seriously ill, about seven miles from Holy Rosary Mission. The boy's family called for help. He needed medical attention, healing. Apparently, two men were called for that day—perhaps there were competing forces at work in the family—and both men came quickly: a *yuwipi* man, or Native healer, and a Jesuit priest.

The *yuwipi* man, Black Elk, was the first to arrive. He came on foot. He must have been close by. Quickly, he pulled out his drum and his tobacco and he started to sing, calling on the spirits to heal the boy from illness. This went on for a while, as the priest made his way there in a horse and buggy.

While in the middle of the intensity of the healing ceremony, Black Elk was interrupted by the priest who, as soon as he arrived, saw what was happening and was appalled. He thought that Black Elk's activity was inappropriate, pagan, and/or antithetical to the Christian ways of healing and salvation that the Society of Jesus were trying to instill in the Lakota on the reservations. The priest was also upset apparently because the boy who was ill was a baptized Catholic—something Black Elk would not have known—giving the priest an even greater sense that there was no place for Lakota *yuwipi* at this particular bedside.

The priest was Joseph Lindebner, SJ, well known in the area. Black Elk would have known him by name.

According to Black Elk's daughter, Lucy Looks Twice, Black Elk's drum and rattle were thrown from the tent, followed by Black Elk himself, as Fr. Joseph screamed, "Satan, get out!"[4] It is with extraordinary humility that Black Elk, then, listened to this black robe—who seems to have been using his position of power with a degree of arrogance and anger to stop the proceedings. Again, Black Elk's daughter Lucy recounts what happened. She must have heard this from her dad:

> My father was really singing away, beating his drum and using his rattle when along came one of the Blackrobes. . . . Father Lindebner had already baptized the boy and had come to give him the last rites. Anyway, he took whatever

my father had prepared on the ground and threw it all into the stove. He took the drum and rattle and threw them outside the tent.

It was then that the Jesuit called Black Elk "Satan," probably quoting the words of Jesus to Peter, whom Jesus thought was trying to stand in his way, in Matthew chapter 16: "He turned and said to Peter, 'Get behind me, Satan! You are a stumbling block to me; for you are setting your mind not on divine things but on human things' " (verse 23).

Lucy continues: "After he got through, [Father Lindebner] came out and saw my father sitting there downhearted and lonely, as though he lost all his powers." The priest encouraged Black Elk to get into his horse and buggy and join him on the ride back to Holy Rosary Mission. Black Elk did. Luci concludes the episode: "My father never talked about the incident but he felt it was Our Lord that appointed or selected him to do the work of the Blackrobes. You might think he was angry, but he wasn't bitter at all."[5]

Black Elk joined the Jesuit on the ride back to Holy Rosary Mission where he then stayed for religious instruction. Perhaps his daughter's account was slightly exaggerated. Some have suggested so. For example, "it was commonly assumed that medicine men such as Black Elk would not allow themselves to be pushed around in that fashion. Similarly, the priest had a reputation for being very kind and gentle."[6] Nevertheless, one remembers the context of the previously mentioned episode in the Gospel of Matthew. It may well be that the words of the priest were unusual for him and that Black Elk's response was unusual for him, and even if so, this would all make perfect sense in the context of a sparking conversion turning into flame.

Two weeks later, at Holy Rosary, Black Elk asked to be baptized. The baptismal name he selected was Nicholas, for the famous fourth-century bishop who inspires the St. Nicholas of Christmas. It may have been de facto selected for him, since the day was December 6. But also, he'd learned that the original Nicholas was most of all known as a healer, which resonated. The way in which this all took place can make people in both the Native and Catholic communities uncomfortable.

Catholic Context on the Reservation

America was an overwhelmingly Protestant country at the turn of the twentieth century. Since the 1840s, Catholic numbers had grown, mostly due to immigration from Ireland and Germany, but by 1900 Catholics still made up only about 15 percent of the total population. (Today the percentage, if you consider all Americans who identify in some way with Catholicism, the number is three times that.) In 1900, America was still very much the land the Puritans had settled. For this reason, Catharine Maria Sedgwick's groundbreaking novel, *Hope Leslie* (1827), could controversially portray Puritan-Indian cross-cultural friendships in a positive light but couldn't see its way to depict Natives' converting to Catholicism with anything but disdain. Even to a critic of traditional Puritan mores like Sedgwick, Catholics were beyond the pale—not to be trusted and even more non-Native (wearing "idolatrous" crucifixes, proponents of "fantastic legends") to the Puritan mindset that dominated the country then. In other words, if Black Elk had wanted to walk a path to easy enculturation and acceptance in the country that surrounded his people, he would have converted to Protestantism, not Catholicism.

The influence of Protestantism was not only felt in American life but in Catholic contexts. At the Vatican, for instance, famous statues by Renaissance artists such as Donatello and Michelangelo were "castrated" in 1857 by order of Pope Pius IX, who thought it was more than immodest to show the full human form. Covering up the private parts with fig leaves, an earlier "solution," was no longer enough. One Native writer, Zitkála-Šá—who was also known as Gertrude Simmons Bonnin, a name given her by the missionaries who taught her in reservation schools—articulates this well when she answers objections she hears from White people about Native dance: "Immodest; the Indians' nudity in the dance is shockingly immodest!" And, "Why! Does he not wear a dress of paint and loin cloth?" She answers that covering up to please outside mores is a kind of false modesty, likening it to "overalls on the soul's improper earthly garment." She goes on: "I wonder how much it would abash God if, for this man's distorted sense, a dress were put on all the marble figures in art museums."[7]

Indians were made to feel increasingly uncomfortable for being Native, more than ever before, during Black Elk's lifetime. But wearing different clothes and carrying different spiritual implements is not what his conversion to Catholicism was about. It was a matter of faith in *Wakan Tanka* as more than Great Spirit—now, too, as God the Father, God the Son, and God the Holy Spirit. "Jesus was not just a good teacher, but the key teacher. Lakota people call Jesus *Wanikiya*, 'He Who Makes Live.' For Black Elk, Jesus and his new life were the answer to a collapsing world: Only he can fully heal the Earth, bring back the dead and explain how to make sense of the newcomers."[8] Also, faith in God became a faith in the sacraments and teachings of the Catholic Church. Nevertheless, for the rest of his life, he would see more continuity than discontinuity between his medicine man work and his catechetical work to come.

As an Indian Christian convert Black Elk was not unusual. The first conversions on the continent took place in the context of Spanish explorers in what is now Florida, led by Ponce de León, more than eighty years before Jamestown in Virginia. The converts were all Native Americans. Also, before Jamestown, in 1542 Franciscan Father Juan de Padilla accompanied Coronado to what is now Kansas, where he met and ministered among the Wichita.

Other prominent Native converts include Samson Occom, who was born a Mohegan and converted to Christianity during the Great Awakening of the 1740s and soon began evangelizing the Pequot on Long Island before seeking ordination as a Presbyterian minister. Occom was one of the cofounders of a new tribe, the Brothertown Indians, that combined Native ways of life with Christian teachings. Occom's life spanned most of the eighteenth century; he died in 1792. Then there was William Apess (or Apes), born and raised a member of the Pequot, who converted to Methodism and then became an itinerate Methodist preacher in New England, always advocating for Native American rights. He died in 1841. There are dozens of other such examples.[9]

Black Elk also wasn't unique in being both a Christian convert and a trained Native holy person (both men and women). There were others such as Catherine Wabose, two generations earlier. She was an Ojibwa holy woman with visions preserved in drawings who converted to Christianity after hearing a Methodist preacher near her home beside Lake Ontario. There were also prominent Native warrior converts among the Lakota, including memorable, iconic figures. Sitting Bull, the famous veteran of the Battle of Little Bighorn, was baptized in 1883. Red Cloud, too, was baptized in 1884 by a Jesuit priest. So there was plenty of precedent for a prominent Native leader to become Catholic. In fact, as every missionary knows, a prudent strategy is to seek out the leaders in a community, working and praying for their conversion, knowing that with the leaders converted, others will follow. What an impact it would have if a holy man among the Lakota were to become a committed Catholic.

Black Elk knew many Christians even as a boy. At nineteen, a year before joining Cody's Wild West Show, he learned about the remarkable Algonquin-Mohawk laywoman, Kateri Tekakwitha ("Kateri" because she was baptized, at nineteen, in honor of St. Catherine of Siena). Kateri, too, lived on a Jesuit mission—in New France, south of Montreal. Black Elk was one of many in the Native community who signed a petition circulating then in support of the cause for her canonization. That cause was officially initiated by the US Council of Catholic Bishops in 1884 and sent to then-Pope Leo XIII, but Kateri was not declared Venerable until 1943. She was canonized in 2012 by Pope Benedict XVI.

Then Black Elk learned more about the faith while traveling in Europe with Wild Bill. He was in frequent contact with many Christians, famous and not, and experienced many churches in European cities, witnessing Christian ritual and teaching in an environment that felt to him different and less fraught with negative precedent from all that he'd known before.

He also had Oglala friends who were Catholics. And there came a point when his work as a medicine man began to feel that it was not enough for him—perhaps even—that it was somehow misguided.

Black Elk wasn't the first in his tribe, or first in his family, to become Catholic. He was, at the time of his conversion, thirty-eight years old. His wife Katie had recently died, and she was a convert to Catholicism herself, given the fact that Black Elk's three sons had also been baptized before their father ever came to the faith.[10] The incident on the night when he was attending a young boy, seeking to heal him, and was rebuked by the Jesuit priest, was the moment of his conversion, but conversions don't have a single moment. As biographer Michael Steltenkamp says, "[I]t is best understood as one incident in a process that had been ongoing for some time."[11]

As we will see in the chapters to come, for Black Elk, "Lakota tradition and Catholicism were not two disparate systems. . . . [T]hey composed one way of looking at the world."[12] This was confusing to many, and it could very well be that we are still unable to fully understand it.

CHAPTER EIGHT

Catechist Nick

One gift of growing up the way Black Elk did was the tremendous facility for memorization he acquired. The Oglala were not an illiterate people. That fiction still exists, perpetuated by Hollywood films that romanticize the era and their people as nobly preliterate.

The word "savage" persisted for centuries as a way for Whites to describe Indigenous people because of preconceived ideas of what civilization meant. Only in recent decades have Catholic bishops begun to apologize to Native communities for scorning their culture and denigrating their practices and ways of life.[1] Before, missionaries would even use "savage" in benevolent contexts, as in, *If the Lakota savage can learn English, our missionaries should be able to learn a little Lakota.* Even Neihardt, in his original preface to *Black Elk Speaks*, points to the word savage as something for the past, until a few pages later when he refers to Black Elk as "illiterate." He wasn't illiterate, except perhaps in English. Neihardt simply never bothered to ask, or consider, how his subject was one of the more articulate communicators in his first language.

Black Elk read and wrote in Lakota, and some English, and probably even a little bit of French. His gift for memorization was due to the way that Oglala children were educated: largely through oral storytelling more than books. He learned much and was able to recall it in ways that would make any person envious.

Soon after his conversion, he needed medical attention for ulcers. He said later that anxiety around his medicine man work had caused these. Whatever the cause, the Jesuits sent him to see doctors, and his condition soon improved. Then they noticed his facility with memorization, recall, and concluded that he would be an excellent teacher. They were right. Nick was identified as having the spiritual gifts of a potential catechist. He was personable. He was well organized. He possessed excellent communication skills. And he had a heart for the Gospel: Good News.

He believed he was improving on his medicine practice by becoming a Catholic. No stranger to healing people, he began to seek to do similar service, only now with the tools of Holy Scripture, prayer, the sign of the cross, and faith in Christ. As an expert in both Lakota and Christian religious systems explains, "Most medicine men view Wakan Tanka as a distinct, single person, who is the Great Grandfather over all. He is the most powerful 'Other' who lives above the heavens."[2] This is about right for Black Elk pre-Catholicism.

It isn't clear to what degree he put away his pipe, drum, and herbs. His daughter Lucy famously declared that after her father "gladly accepted the faith on December 6, 1904. . . . He put all his medicine practice away."[3] But Lucy's account of what happened to her father contains other odd details that have been questioned over the years, so we're not entirely sure. He never spoke of that day when he was tossed out of the tent by the priest, but he spoke later about his Catholic faith in unequivocal terms. He found a seamless transition from praying to spirits, as he'd long done in his *yuwipi* practice, to appealing to the Holy Spirit. As the petition to open Black Elk's canonization, written by his great-grandchildren, recently summarized:

> Believing that *Wakantanka*, the Great Spirit, called him to greater service, he became a Christian and practiced his Lakota ways as well as the Catholic religion. He was comfortable praying with his pipe and his rosary and participated in Mass and Lakota ceremonies on a regular basis.[4]

He also married again. His first wife, Katie, had died about eighteen months before the December incident attending to the boy in the tipi. Now, in his first year as a committed Catholic—which was Katie's own religious practice—he married a woman whom he had known in the Pine Ridge community: Anna Brings White. She too had been married before, and she too was a Catholic. She was also a widow and had two daughters.

Together they built a nurturing home for faith, their children, and all who came to visit. They were generous with their hospitality. Anna was warm and welcoming. She loved to sing hymns; and with Black Elk, the family would often pray together. She joined the St. Mary's Society for Christian women at Pine Ridge. Nine years later, she would give birth to a son, and they named him Nick Jr.

An Apostolic Ministry

Nick Black Elk's success as a catechist came at a time when the church was focusing its missions throughout the world on raising converts—particularly among Native populations where Christianity was recent or new—for the purpose of building indigenously led parishes. The feeling among Oglala Catholics at that time was similar to what it must have been to one of the early Christians gathered around St. Paul or one of the other apostles in the first century. A catechist and healer like Nicholas Black Elk would take responsibility for a district, build a small chapel, begin to preach and teach with simple tools such as Bibles and hymnbooks of praises, and one by one converts would follow. They would be baptized, and the called-out ones would grow in small but dedicated numbers.

Black Elk began to work closely with the Jesuits at Pine Ridge, learning from them. It must have been clear to every Oglala that a man of great spiritual stature, a leader whom they trusted, was now discovering the ways of the Christian *Wanikiya*, "Savior." He learned to read Lakota with greater skill and rapidly became known for that remarkable ability to memorize Holy Scripture in the Lakota language.

His expansive understanding of the world around him spilled into his teaching of the Bible and into his instruction of new converts to the faith. He saw the world similarly to how he had seen it all along: as a gift of the Creator, who is in control of all things, and who loves his people. But his new faith brought him a deeper sense of sin, as well as a biblical understanding of how and why human beings are, by their very nature, sinful. The Lakota understanding of human beings was as weak and powerless compared to the world around them—and compared to the Great Spirit—but in Black Elk this now became a Christian understanding of human beings as separated from God because of sin, with clear ways of repairing the damage that was done and following Christ through to repair.

St. Agnes Chapel, Manderson

Manderson, South Dakota—at Pine Ridge Reservation—became his district of primary responsibility, and he built a chapel there for Mass to be held whenever the priest came through. He named it St. Agnes Chapel. It was finished in

1906. There, Nick assisted Fr. Lindebner at Mass, as did other catechists-in-training, including Paul Catches and Tom Yellow Bull, whose names are also still remembered today among the Lakota at Pine Ridge. They were paid anywhere from $5 to $15 each month, and the Jesuits were constantly seeking additional sources of support for what was a growing ministry and need.

The responsibilities of a catechist were many and varied. Priests were few, and they had to travel long distances to keep in contact with everyone in their parish, often able to celebrate Mass only once a month in most places. This is where the catechists became essential:

> Since the circuit took a month to complete, the Jesuits could offer Mass in each community only once a month. On the other Sundays the catechists held the service at which they preached, read the gospel, and led the people in prayers and hymns in Lakota. During Lent, the catechists went to the houses of each Catholic family to pray and say the rosary. Also in this season, they gathered the laity in the chapels, sometimes five times a week, and made the stations of the cross. They also counseled people who had marital troubles. . . . Of course, the catechists also taught the children as well as the adults about the Catholic Church, and also tried to convert non-Catholics.[5]

Catechists also conducted funeral services, and they were often at people's bedsides when they were ill. Nick Black Elk knew very well how the Lakota looked to spiritual leaders at those times in their lives. Personal visits and simply being present with others in times of need were part of Lakota life. Often, these visits took days, not hours.

He soon became known for his dynamic preaching and teaching. Like his skills for storytelling and memorizing, he possessed an extraordinary understanding of the importance of sign and symbol in people's lives, and his sermons were marked by concise and tangible applications that related closely to the life of the Oglala. Photographs of Black Elk standing among other Oglala catechists show them all in Western dress (coats and ties), but sometimes Black Elk is still wearing his moccasins.

In 1919, Pope Benedict VI wrote an apostolic letter "to the Patriarchs, Primates, Archbishops and Bishops of the Catholic world on the activity carried out by the missionaries in the world"; in this document, *Maximum Illud*, he said: "Those who preside over the Mission must address their primary concern to the good formation of the Native clergy, on which the best hopes of the new Christianity are especially placed. In fact the Indigenous priest, having common with his countrymen the origin, the nature, the mentality and the aspirations, is wonderfully suitable to instill in their hearts the Faith, because more than any other knows the ways of persuasion. Therefore it often happens that he comes easily where the foreign missionary can not reach."[6]

Then, in 1926, Pope Pius XI wrote an encyclical on the subject, *Rerum Ecclesiae*. In that document, speaking to missionaries, he said:

> Perhaps it would be well if you would consider . . . if it would not be more advantageous all around to establish entirely new Congregations, which would correspond better with the genius and character of the natives and which would be more in keeping with the needs and the spirit of the different countries.
>
> We cannot pass over in silence another point most important for the spread of the gospel, namely, the necessity of increasing the number of catechists. Catechists may be Europeans, or preferably natives, who help the missionaries in their work especially by instructing and preparing

catechumens for baptism. . . . In this catechetical work
their success will be in exact proportion to the intimate
knowledge which they possess of the mental ability and
habits of the natives.[7]

So Nicholas Black Elk was exactly what the church was
hoping for.

A Catechist's Tool Kit

During his decades as a busy catechist among the Lakota,
the Jesuits published the first Lakota prayer and hymnbook.
Printed in 1927 in Germany and distributed widely on the
US reservations, Nick made good use of it. Every prayer
popular among Catholics everywhere, plus gospel readings
for the Sundays in Advent, Lent, and Easter, were part of
this pocket-sized book for everyday use. Catholic piety was
by then thoroughly in the Lakota language. For example:

> The Pater Noster—was on page 25
> *Ateunyanpi mahpiya ekta nanke kin*
> ("Our Father who art in heaven")

> From The Gloria—was on page 18
> *Iyotan wankatu ekta Wakantanka wowitan yuha ni*
> ("Glory to God in the highest")

Black Elk once said: "I say in my own Sioux Lakota language: *Ateunyanpi*: Our Father who art in heaven, hallowed
be thy name—as Christ taught us to say."[8] These books and
others like them were prepared by Jesuits at the Rosebud
and Pine Ridge Reservations who worked closely with Black
Elk. It and other resources were part of his tool kit.

Missionaries also provided Native catechists with "pictorial catechisms," which were colorful representations of
Christian symbols, such as the cross, sacraments, and saints,

along with images of Jesus Christ and God the Father. Some of these were referred to as "Ladder catechisms," since they were organized vertically, showing the way to God in heaven. Nicholas Black Elk often used ladder catechisms. But the preferred Jesuit one was developed by members of the Missionary Oblates of Mary Immaculate (OMI) in nearby Canada and called "The Two Roads" catechism.

Two Roads catechism showed an ordinary road that leads through life without God and to the side of it, the more blessed and sacred path of journeying on the road with Christ, with the cross in view, and God and heaven awaiting one at the end of the journey. The sacred path was called "The Good Red Road of Jesus," and the ordinary road was labeled "The Black Road of Difficulties." Both roads showed the Old and New Testaments of the Bible as revealing the "good" and the "bad" ways to follow. The bad way was a path from the Garden of Eden through Cain to the Tower of Babel and on through other instances of rebellion against God, toward hell. The good way also began in the Garden but moved through Noah's Ark, other instances of faithfulness, to the seven sacraments of the church, the seven virtues, toward the promise of heaven. This is the tool that Nick most often utilized as a tool to share his Catholic faith with people who could not read the new Lakota-translated Scriptures and other tools. They were also effective with children, who were naturally drawn to the use of pictorial images.

Nick often used his rosary to teach both children and adults, as well. He would hold the cross in his hand and describe its importance. Then he would work through the cruciform beads and the decades, explaining how to pray and what to say. It was Pope Leo XIII, the holy pontiff who died the summer before Black Elk's conversion, who was "The Rosary Pope." He wrote twelve encyclicals and five apostolic exhortations on the subject, saying: "The Rosary is the most excellent form of prayer and the most efficacious means of attaining eternal life. It is the remedy for all our evils, the root of all our blessings. There is no more excellent way of praying." Not only was this the most popular form of prayer for Catholics, but it contained a summary of the faith, as well as assurance of remedy against trials, temptations, and hardships.

Not unlike St. Paul in the first century, Nick also began writing and dictating letters of spiritual exhortation and advice that were distributed widely among his people at Pine Ridge and elsewhere and sometimes published in the local Jesuit-run Lakota newspaper, *Sinasapa Wocekiye Taenanpaha*, "Black Robe Church Paper." Here is a portion of one letter from November 12, 1906:

> Since the last Sioux Congress and at the present time, I have visited the Rosebud Reservation. The people there told me that they want churches built on their own districts. I was pleased to hear these people are interested in God. As I was present there, they took up a collection for me, and these people donated to me.
> . . . I thank these people for doing a great deed for me. . . . I spoke mainly on Jesus—when he was on earth, the teachings and his sufferings. I myself do a lot of these things. I suffer and I try to teach my people the things that I wanted them to learn, but it's never done.[9]

Another letter a year later expressed a sense of urgency. Even as a new catechist, he sensed that fervor for the Catholic faith was generationally driven and might not last beyond him and those of his generation:

> God the Father, and Jesus Christ—I pray to them often St. Joseph's and St. Mary's Society will never fade away. Some day this is going to happen: because the present generation

is beginning to turn. But let us train our younger ones to continue on the work that we've been doing. I'm very old now, and my days are numbered.

. . . My friends and relatives I speak to you from the bottom of my heart. Please try and do the things that we're supposed to do. Let us not forget the main person—that is Wakan Tanka. And the priest or the bishop has told us never to be afraid because God is always with us.[10]

He even interpreted world events for those in his pastoral care; for instance, soon after the Titanic sank in the North Atlantic, Catechist Nick wrote this for those who read the Catholic newspaper:

Men of the United States constructed a very large and fast boat. We made many millions of dollars, so that in a few nights, one crossed the ocean. . . . They said never would the boat sink. . . . Yes, those rich men believed it. They did not know what they would come up against. So, one day they struck against something, so the boat they made sank from blindness, a difficulty that came over them, and their fright was great.

He was probably reflecting not only on Holy Scripture and the Christian life but on his own experiences of having traveled by ship along that northern Atlantic course. He went on:

Yes my Relatives, take a look. There was an accident due to a great honor. The trouble with the world's honor is that the trouble is up above. In worldly honor we twitch. You pay your debts up above when you are up against something. You do not see when you are struck by something large. You wander about, a ghost that will wander about and sinks. There is a grave sin here. Then you will say: "Lord, Lord!" You will say: "That is very troublesome, my

Relatives." Desire to be close to our Savior. Desire to stay in our ship.[11]

There were many health and family concerns, too, during these years. Tuberculosis was present in Black Elk's lungs for decades, and he occasionally went to hot springs for treatments. He also worried about his children. Son Johnnie, from his first marriage, died in 1909. Several years later, Black Elk was concerned about his son Ben, whom he seems to have worried would not find what he needed on the reservation, so Nick and Anna sent Ben to a boarding school for Indian children in Carlisle, Pennsylvania. While Ben was there, his father worried that he might not faithfully attend Mass.[12]

His correspondence also included frequent updates to his Jesuit superiors, offering reports of progress and discussing difficulties encountered in his work. One letter to the monsignor in charge of the Bureau of Catholic Indian Missions reported: "I have had a number join our flock and I expect I have quite a number more in the future but I am in a critical condition at present [referring to his health]. Therefore I gave [sic] you thanks in Christ and wish for you to remember me in your prayers. I am now going to make my way to Hot Springs for a treatment." He refers to the hot springs that emanate from what was then, and still is, Hot Springs, South Dakota, very near Pine Ridge Reservation, said to have healing powers for many ailments. The letter concludes: "I beg you to find me a little help and would like to hear of you too and if our Savior gives me help on my sickness . . . I will again look into our business among my Catholic Sioux's."[13]

His work was, in fact, funded by the Bureau of Catholic Indian Missions, headquartered in Washington, DC, to reach beyond his own Pine Ridge Reservation. It must have been strange for him to work with leaders in Washington. Beginning in 1908, they sent him to Wyoming, Nebraska, and other reservations in the Dakotas, where he ministered as a traveling catechist of extraordinary ability.

Five years later and then for a few years running, he served all the way across the state of South Dakota—250 miles to the east—at the Yankton Reservation, working closely with a Jesuit priest, Father Westropp, well known at Pine Ridge and Holy Rosary, who was then sent by his religious order to Poona, India, to open schools. Black Elk understood the culture of missions and missionaries and was one among them.

When Fr. Westropp left, other Jesuits took his place on the reservations and in assisting and supervising Nick in his catechetical work. For three more decades he worked with many, including, most notably, Father Eugene Buechel, SJ. A German-born priest who worked at Holy Rosary Mission and Pine Ridge Reservation for half a century, Buechel was also a trained linguist and anthropologist. He was the priest who presided at the funeral of Red Cloud in 1909. It is his work in translating Lakota that is the backbone for the standard Lakota-English dictionary still used today.[14] He was younger than Black Elk by seven years and outlived him by four. In the words of one of the vice-postulators of the cause for canonization of Nicholas Black Elk, Fr. Buechel was "one of the last fluent Lakota-speaking Jesuits who seamlessly presented Christianity in Lakota. Now, monolingual American-born Jesuits prevailed, who were less immersed in Lakota language and culture and more insistent on following the church's Roman-centric rules."[15]

CHAPTER NINE

Baffling Two Communities

As we've already seen, many Lakota have sought to distance their kinsman from the White man's religion, regardless of what he said about it himself. Wallace Black Elk, for instance, writes about Lakota shamanism and Black Elk's legacy, saying that Black Elk's *yuwipi* practice ran far deeper than did his Catholicism. And in the preface to Wallace Black Elk's book, William Lyon, his translator, says, "[M]any scholars believe Black Elk stopped his shamanic practice around 1904, when he was baptized a Catholic. I have reason to believe he continued on in secret."[1]

And then we see our subject, Nicholas Black Elk himself, saying this in what was transcribed by Joseph Epes Brown:

> We have been told by the white men, or at least by those who are Christian, that God sent to men His son, who would restore order and peace upon the earth; and we have been told that Jesus the Christ was crucified, but that he shall come again at the Last Judgment, the end of this world or cycle. This I understand and know that it is true, but the white men should know that for the red people

too, it was the will of *Wakan-Tanka*, the Great Spirit, that an animal turn itself into a two-legged person in order to bring the most holy pipe to His people; and we too were taught that this White Buffalo Cow Woman who brought our sacred pipe will appear again at the end of this "world," a coming which we Indians know is now not very far off.

He doesn't exactly sound like a convinced Catholic, like a renowned catechist.

A moment later, about the sacred pipe he adds: "Most people call it a 'peace pipe,' yet now there is no peace on earth or even between neighbors, and I have been told that it has been a long time since there has been peace in the world. There is much talk of peace among the Christians, yet this is just talk. Perhaps it may be, and this is my prayer that, through our sacred pipe . . . peace may come to those peoples who can understand, an understanding which must be of the heart and not of the head alone. Then they will realize that we Indians know the One true God, and that we pray to Him continually."[2]

So you can see why people in both the Native and Catholic communities are often confused about Nicholas Black Elk— who he was and where his loyalties lay.

* * *

Christians who are troubled by Black Elk's conversion seem to expect that he will disdain his Native background in ways that he clearly did not. They seem upset that he did not see more disconnections between his medicine man practice and his catechetical one. Those who are disappointed in the quality of his conversion perhaps fit the characterization of the writer V. S. Naipaul, who when writing about the evan-

gelists among Indigenous people in South America, re-
marked: "The missionary must first teach self-contempt."[3]
This is one of the vestiges of colonialism: a complete dep-
recation of Native ways, seemingly, in order to make room
for Christian faith.

On the other hand, there are those occasions when Nicholas Black Elk set the record straight, clarifying the sincerity
and totality of his Catholic faith. Some of these statements
have had trouble meeting the light of day.

Even his enthusiasm for the Ghost Dance was sometimes
seen by Black Elk through a Christian lens. He told this to
John Neihardt, describing a vision he had while doing the
Dance, but then Neihardt didn't include it in his book: "It
seemed as though there were wounds in the palms of his
hands. It seems to me on thinking it over that I have seen
the son of the Great Spirit himself."[4] None of this fits the
narrative of the life of Black Elk as told by Neihardt—so
much so that Black Elk's most recent long-form biographer
doesn't accept it. The vision of Black Elk as the remnant of
a monoculture is simply too appealing to give up. Rather
than acknowledge that Neihardt's agenda was anti-Chris-
tian, biographer Joe Jackson tells readers that Catholicism
was unimportant to Black Elk; it was only a sort of dressing
and didn't affect the one, continuous spiritual vision of
Black Elk's life: "Was he still Catholic when Neihardt drove
up, or using the Church as a blind to return to the hold and
outlawed ways?" argues Jackson.[5]

Wallace Black Elk and Joe Jackson aren't the only naysay-
ers. There is also one of Black Elk's great-granddaughters,
Charlotte Black Elk. After the cause for her great-grandfather's
canonization was formalized, she told an interviewer: "In
the family, we have stories of them trying to baptize him,
and him hiding under a bed, and a priest pouring a bucket

of water on him and pronouncing him baptized." She said that she believes he was never really a Catholic, because he was Lakota, and Lakota religion, not Catholicism, is what was in his blood.[6]

* * *

But these accounts simply don't fit the facts of the second half of Nicholas Black Elk's life or his teachings, as revealed in the letters he wrote or dictated over forty-five years as a Catholic catechist. Charlotte Black Elk's great-grandfather's words tell a different story from what she said to the interviewer. Nick Black Elk's decades as a catechist and his missionary trips to other reservations, which he called "spiritual scalping-tours," were filled with teaching the Gospel of Jesus Christ. He was a missionary to his own people, working in partnership with black robes as well as other Natives who were Catholics.

Toward the end of his life he wrote:

> For the last thirty years I have lived very differently from what the white man told about me. I am a believer. The Catholic priest Short Father baptized me thirty years ago. From then on they have called me Nick Black Elk. Very many of the Indians know me. Now I have converted and live in the true faith of God the Father, the Son, and the Holy Spirit. Accordingly, I say in my own Sioux Indian language, "Our Father, who art in heaven, hallowed be thy name," as Christ taught us and instructed us to say. I say the Apostle's Creed and I believe it all.

He goes on in this document, which he signed in 1934, intending it as a final testament, clarifying for people who he was, especially after the publication of *Black Elk Speaks*:

I send my people on the straight road that Christ's church has taught us about. While I live I will never fall from faith in Christ.

Thirty years ago I knew little about the one we call God. At that time I was a very good dancer. In England I danced before our Grandmother, Queen Victoria. At that time I gave medicines to the sick. Perhaps I was proud, I considered myself brave and I considered myself to be a good Indian, but now I think I am better.

St. Paul also became better after his conversion. I know that the Catholic religion is good, better than the Sun dance or the Ghost dance. Long ago the Indians performed such dances only for glory. They cut themselves and caused the blood to flow. But for the sake of sin Christ was nailed on the cross to take our sins away. The Indian religion of long ago did not benefit mankind. The medicine men sought only glory and presents from their curing. Christ commanded us to be humble and He taught us to stop sin. The Indian medicine men did not stop sin. Now I despise sin. And I want to go straight in the righteous way that the Catholics teach us so my soul will reach heaven. This is the way I wish it to be. With a good heart I shake hands with all of you.[7]

This testament was witnessed by his daughter, Lucy, and by Father Joseph A. Zimmerman, a Jesuit friend and mentor. Despite the ways that he remained a giant among his people in Native ways of spiritual understanding, he seems to have unequivocally realized that salvation was achieved through the Son of God as preached by the priests of Pine Ridge.

There was another document also dictated by him at that time—just after he'd recovered from a serious injury and was contemplating the end of his life. In this one, he disavows Neihardt's book because it did not make mention of his Christian faith. It includes these lines:

> I trusted him and finished the story of my life for him. . . .
> I also asked to put at the end of this story that I was not a
> pagan but have been converted into the Catholic Church in
> which I work as a Catechist for more than 25 years. I've quit
> all these pagan works. But he didn't mention [these] last talks.
>
> So if they can't put this Religion life in the last part of
> that Book . . . I ask you my dear friends that this Book of
> my life will be null & void. Because I value my soul more
> than my Body. I'm awful sorry for the mistake I've made.[8]

We've seen the melancholy of Black Elk looking back on
the changes and loss that his people experienced: land and
hegemony gone, freedom to move and hunt and live as they
wish, vanished. But his melancholy was about more than
these losses. The sadness he felt in his sixties, when his story
first reached a White audience, was two generations removed from the Massacre at Wounded Knee, when the
changes he'd seen had expanded to a broad secularization
that went beyond Lakota religion and ritual. He also felt
that his people were lost and wandering and that the losses
weren't only about land and ways of life but about what
Christians refer to as a need for salvation.

It was mostly in the area of ethics that Black Elk made
changes in his life after becoming a Catholic. The second
greatest commandment, according to Jesus, is to love your
neighbor as yourself, and this was foreign to Lakota ways.
Most of the Beatitudes, as well, struck the Lakota as coun-
terintuitive or even ethically improper. Loving one's enemies
made no sense in the tribal wars and Native manner of
handling disputes. There was even virtue in murder, in some
cases, in Lakota ethical ways, if to demonstrate bravery or
manhood, which were themselves virtues.

As a catechist, Nick taught that some of these old ethical
ways should be replaced by the new ways of Jesus. One
could say: "When Black Elk became a Catholic, he converted

from a tribal religion to a universal religion."[9] Even so, it was commonplace for Whites to commit atrocities on Native people, despite their supposed commitment to the values of Jesus. The actions of the majority of "Christians" usually destroyed any notion of Christian love that White missionaries were trying to teach. Whites made it all too easy for the ethical principles of the new universal religion of Christianity to be seen as insincere.

He Anticipated a New Catholic Openness

The complexity of Nick Black Elk's religious life was an anticipation and a foretaste of what would happen in the Catholic Church worldwide a generation later at the Second Vatican Council (1962–65). At Vatican II, the world's Catholic bishops wrote a document called *Nostra Aetate*, which means "In Our Time." The bishops called it a "Declaration on the Relation of the Church to Non-Christian Religions." Paragraph 2 states:

> The Catholic Church rejects nothing that is true and holy in these religions.

What a shock this was to many of the faithful—and still is—that there can be truth and holiness in other religions. Also, what changes this declaration wrought in the methods and purposes of Catholic missionaries throughout the world! But it would have made good sense to Black Elk, his Christian Lakota friends and family, and even to most of the Jesuits who taught him and worked alongside him at Pine Ridge and Holy Rosary.

As Professor Ross Enochs of Marist College has shown:

> One of the reasons the Catholic missions were so successful was that Catholicism was structurally similar to Native

84 *Catechist*

American religion. . . . The Lakotas' views of rituals,
helper spirits, the dead, justification, salvation, and recon-
ciliation were similar to Catholic beliefs, and the Jesuits
used these similarities to draw the Lakotas to the Catholic
Church.[10]

Nick Black Elk brought Lakota and Catholic spiritual
practice, belief, and ritual into a way of faith that was mostly
uninterrupted. He had invoked God's presence scores of
times before becoming a Christian, and he would continue
to do so after his conversion, with only different changes in
language and tone.

He had an understanding of God's power in the world—
and in a human life—before his conversion, as well as after
his conversion, and the differences were minor. The Great
Spirit, *Wakantanka*, was the object of his devotion, and the
Great Spirit, *Wakantanka*, seen through the lens of God the
Father, would continue to be his devotion.

One evidence for this continuity can be found in early
Jesuit missionary practice. When the Jesuits first learned
about Lakota ways of life and ritual, they realized the Lakota were already monotheists, and so urged them to keep
praying to *Wakantanka*, God. They saw no need for them
to unlearn, only to expand, how they expressed devotion to
the Holy One. They did not practice V. S. Naipaul's teaching
of "self-contempt." In this way, a Jesuit educator at Holy
Rosary Mission in 1928 could record: "367 Sioux Indian
boys and girls are being taught to know and love *Wakan
Tanka*, the Great Spirit."[11]

There were exceptions to this cohesion. During Nick's
time as a catechist, the bishop of Lead—which is now Rapid
City—wrote a letter addressed to "the Catholic Indians" of
the diocese in which he advises them, as a "good shepherd"

protecting his flock "from danger," to avoid all use of in-toxicating drink, to shun divorce, and not to dance. "Danc-ing and all the Old Customs of the Indians, because they are used by the devil to put what is bad into the mind and the heart of him who takes part in these practices," is a custom to be removed from one's life entirely.[12] We know that Nick didn't always follow this guideline; but to do other than what one's bishop advises has, of course, always been a Catholic commonplace. He came to view the Sun Dance, for instance, in light of Christian asceticism—so alike it was, and is, to a Lenten fasting practice of prayer. During Black Elk's final two decades, there were often Indian dances sanc-tioned by the Jesuits, taking place at Holy Rosary Mission.[13]

Both Lakota and Catholic understand the presence of God or Great Spirit in the world around them. This is global as well as personal. Both communities believe in the afterlife and the presence of ancestors or saints, as intercessors for the still living, from the world to come.

Ross Enochs summarizes a few more important parallels in these sentences:

> Lakotas and Catholics also stressed that works and faith were both necessary for salvation. For Catholics and La-kotas salvation was not only a matter of having the correct beliefs but also a matter of practicing these beliefs in the world. Also related to their conception of works was their conception of reconciliation. The Lakotas gave gifts to atone for misdeeds, and similarly, Catholics did penance to help make up for the effects of the sins they committed.[14]

Even dreams and visions have a shared importance in both traditions. Nick didn't see reason to disconnect from his vi-sion life after converting to Catholicism. Lucy Looks Twice, his daughter, once explained her father's faith this way:

> [My father] and Father Buechel would talk. They talked about my father's visions . . . and the Sun Dance, and all the Indian ceremonies that my father said were connected to Christianity. My father said we were like the Israelites, the Jews, waiting for Christ.[15]

For all these reasons, it is understandable that Nick Black Elk's life was confusing to many people. It is frankly still confusing—because despite all the decades and centuries that have gone by and the many examples of people who have lived as faithful Christians while maintaining a strong connection to another religious system or tradition of ritual, we haven't come very far in attempting to understand how this works.

Was Black Elk a true Lakota in the second half of his life? Yes. David Treuer, an Ojibwe from the Leech Lake Reservation in Minnesota and a 2019 National Book Award finalist, probably says it best:

> Many Indians prefer not to think about Black Elk's later years and consider his conversion as a kind of surrender, a confirmation that the old ways were in fact dead. Maybe, maybe not. Black Elk was determined to live and to adapt. That doesn't make him less of an Indian, as I see it; it makes him more of one.[16]

Was he also a real Christian? Yes.

PART THREE

SAINT

CHAPTER TEN

Quiet Days at Last

One could almost chart Nicholas Black Elk's life in 40-year periods, as preachers have long done for the biblical Moses. Moses lived to be 120: 40 years as a slave and prince in Egypt, 40 years of meeting God in the burning bush and tending sheep, and 40 years leading his people toward the Promised Land. Black Elk spent his first 40 or so years in a life that might seem separated from the life he then lived in his final 40 or so. Quite different from each other, the first 40 were marked by adventure, travel, and violence—while the final 40 years were, by comparison, very quiet.

His health was poor. He suffered from tuberculosis, a disease that ravaged Native American communities throughout Black Elk's lifetime, since at least 1912. Smallpox, pneumonia, measles, and whooping cough were common on the reservations, but no disease was more devastating to Indigenous people than TB. Before contracting the "coughing sickness" Black Elk watched three of his sons die of it, as well as his sister. He sent two of his children away to boarding schools where they avoided contracting it. The debate is ongoing as to whether Whites were the ones to introduce

TB into Native communities; even if they were not directly culpable, the poverty, poor nutrition, and harsh living conditions forced upon Indigenous people on reservations made contracting TB far more likely. As late as 2008, Native Americans were more than five times likelier to have tuberculosis than non-Hispanic Whites.[1]

Throughout the second half of his life, Black Elk would often sit beside those who were struggling with coughing sickness and offer comfort as well as medicinal remedies. In fact, his own contraction of the illness may have been similar to how some historians have tried to explain the stigmata wounds of St. Francis of Assisi as leprous: were they a direct result of his passionate work among the sick? Such compassion and self-renunciation in the service of loving one's neighbor is indeed miraculous.

There were other ailments too. John Neihardt referred often to Black Elk's near-blindness, beginning at the time of their first interview—he was "staring upon the ground with half blind eyes. . . . [H]e was almost blind."[2] Then, less than two years later: "Recently he has become totally [blind], a fact of which he informed me quite casually and apparently without sense of affliction." One of Black Elk's biographers explains that this happened as the result of "corneal flash burns suffered during either a *yuwipi* or a *heyoka* ceremony. In one account, Black Elk and Kills Enemy pushed a cartridge into the ground to create some small explosive effects during a *heyoka* ceremony. But when they tamped the shell flush, it exploded into Black Elk's eyes."[3] This must have taken place in the first forty years of his life—not between the summer of 1930, when Neihardt first arrived at Pine Ridge, and early 1932, when he wrote, "Recently he has become totally [blind]." But the Lakota medicine man who saw Queen Victoria, the nightlife of Paris, and the massacre of Wounded Knee was significantly less able to see much at all during the four decades he spent as a Catholic.

The sense of a wise, aging Native leader at the end of his life, relaying wisdom rapidly vanishing from view, was essential to the commercial success of *Black Elk Speaks* and has become a fundamental metaphor through which we view Native people still today. The elderly Indigenous man or woman who stares into the distance, absent to the moment, but pregnant with thoughts and memories of the past, has become a stereotype.

The second half of Black Elk's life was full of travels—only more localized than before—sermons, teaching, study, and care for his fellow Lakota and members of many other tribes and congregations, as he pursued the active life of a catechist. He was earnestly studying the Scriptures, reading them in Lakota translation. He had poor eyesight, Black Elk's daughter Lucy said, "but he learned to read Scripture and prayer books in the Indian language." Jesuit priests supervising his work confirmed this. One of them wrote: "[B]y some hook or crook [he has] learned how to read, and he knows his religion thoroughly."[4]

His passion for evangelism was evident in the results of his work. A young priest, Fr. Henry Westropp, recently assigned to Pine Ridge, said of Black Elk: "In his neighborhood, conversion follows conversion, and the Black Gown [Westropp, a Jesuit] had all he could do to follow in the trail broken by the earnest neophyte."[5] This doesn't sound like a blind wisdom teacher staring off into the distance, searching for answers in the past. Black Elk was traveling widely, preaching often, and stirring up conversions to the delight of the priests throughout the area.

Since the time of his conversion, he had had a keen sense of the hope of heaven. This was natural for a man who had suffered as much as he had and who understood so well the pain and suffering of generations of his people. In a letter from July 15, 1909, Black Elk wrote:

> I have seen a number of different people—the ordinary people living on this earth—the Arapaho, the Shoshoni, the Omaha, the tribe living in California and Florida, the Rosebud, the Cheyenne River Sioux tribe, the Standing Rock, and our own, the Oglalas. The White men living in all these places—I have said prayers for their tribe. I'm really moved that I was able to travel to those places and meet people that are very friendly. . . . We all suffer in this land. But let me tell you, God has a special place for us when our time has come.[6]

So these weren't all quiet days.

Fr. Westropp and other Whites often compared him, with wonder, to St. Paul among the Indians. His industry and enthusiasm were that great. So where did the quiet come from? These years were simpler for him, without the foreign travel, without the intrigue and ambiguity of being a Lakota with public fanfare, without the danger of warring conflict, with less pressure put upon him by wife and children, and without the questioning and self-doubt as to who he was and what purpose his life held.

Nick was busy working for his people, which often included lobbying the Jesuits for more resources. Sometimes these requests were misunderstood, and he was subject to old prejudices. Once, for instance, when he sent a request to a monsignor for money to help fund his growing work, the monsignor asked Fr. Westropp for advice and Westropp, who might have known better, responded: "To make him one present would plant a weed in his soul. . . . Begging has become a passion with many of these fellows."[7] This was a common perspective of Whites, including presidents Washington, Jefferson, and Jackson, among others, whose quotes on the matter are easily found. It is more likely that Catholic catechist Indians were always asking for more because the people whom they served were always in need of more.

He had to work harder than any White catechist did to prove himself. This is almost always true of the person of color, the immigrant, and the stranger. Black Elk *did* work harder. The analogy to St. Paul is not far-fetched—even if the black robes saw their new convert as like St. Paul, who had once been Saul, working in opposition to the church that he now endeavored so eagerly to aid.[8] Black Elk had to work harder than others to show the sincerity of his faith, and despite his efforts, he still had trouble, at times, convincing some of his closest coreligionists that he was one of them. Just three years before his death, in 1947, the Benedictine sister and scholar (*Beginnings of Catholicism in South Dakota*, 1943), Sr. Mary Claudia Duratschek, could use this analogy to say, "[L]ike a second St. Paul, Black Elk went around trying to convert his tribesmen whom, before his conversion, he had helped shackle in the fetters of paganism."[9] Even the most knowledgeable had trouble understanding.

In 1942, his beloved wife Anna died. By then, his active catechetical work had wound down, his age and health making frequent travel and activity difficult. One of his priest friends at Pine Ridge tells us:

> Old age, blindness and the seven miles between him and the nearest Catholic church prevent him from often hearing Mass, so at times I promise to say Mass at his home. Then he sends out word and gathers in the entire neighborhood, and as in his old-time catechist days leads them in hymns and prayers.[10]

Nick returned to remembering the old Indian ways of life through performance—starting the "Sitting Bull Indian Pageant" with some friends in 1934. Rather than leave behind the "Wild West" days entirely, he became a performer again. He put on what was now a costume, rather than his daily dress, dancing and recreating the rituals of Oglala life for paying audiences. Each summer until his death, Black Elk was there in Sitting Bull Caverns, nine miles south of Rapid City, South Dakota, with his family and friends, beating his drum, leading pipe ceremonies, and chanting. He had commercial intentions—to reach the tourists who were now flooding into the area to see Mount Rushmore (officially completed on October 31, 1941)—but he was also demonstrating that a medicine man and a catechist can be two, not disparate, parts of one life story.

He became a bridge between cultures, accepting invitations to visit Rushmore, a monument that was not easily accepted or even acknowledged by many of his fellow Oglala, since to them it represented only the White person's colonization of Native land. But Nick was there in 1936, accompanied by reporters, as the head of Thomas Jefferson was about to be unveiled, and he asked and received permission to perform Oglala rituals. As would be reported in the Rapid City *Daily Journal* on August 28:

> He prayed for the preservation of his people and for "unity of my people and the whites in the name of brotherhood," that Borglum [the sculptor of the monument] and his men be protected in their work. He also called attention of the gods to the need of rain, and asked that "greenness and abundance" be forthcoming. He called for preservation of the greatness of the memories of the men whose granite likenesses are being carved on the mountain, and asked

that their greatness be carried on through "changes of nations and races."[11]

He wasn't praying to "the gods." On this detail the reporter misunderstood Black Elk. But it was difficult for a reporter—let alone many of the Jesuit fathers at Pine Ridge and elsewhere in 1936—to understand that an Oglala's devotion to *Wakan Tanka* was not interrupted but expanded when he became a Roman Catholic. Continuing this tradition, beginning in the years immediately following Black Elk's death, Benjamin Black Elk became such a fixture at Rushmore that he became known as the "fifth face of Mount Rushmore," often posing for government and commercial photographs, dressed in full Oglala ceremonial costume, remembering his father's embracing of the place.

Was He a Saint?

It was a special combination of qualities that set Nicholas Black Elk apart from other people. Neihardt wrote in his original preface: "Black Elk may fairly be described as a saint in the deeper meaning of that term, as signifying a rare form of genius."[12] He was probably right about that. He went on to explain that Black Elk's personality could be brooding and his disposition melancholy but that he was also exceedingly kind and cheerful. Neihardt wanted to portray a man who stood apart from the White man's religion, which is why he ignored Black Elk's Catholicism, and yet he still used the language of sanctity that's indebted to Catholic teaching. He didn't know how prescient he was.

Nor did Black Elk's most recent biographer, whose telling of the life also lacks any sensitivity to Catholicism, grasp this. Yet this biographer (over)states in his prologue: "many consider him [Black Elk] the only true American holy man to come out of the twentieth century."[13] We know better; there have been others. But we also now have a fuller picture of who Nicholas Black Elk was.

He died at home on August 17, 1950, after receiving last rites, his incredible life spanning from the Indian wars of Ulysses S. Grant until the years of the Cold War.

His health had deteriorated greatly in those final years. A fall on winter ice caused a broken hip, following by hospitalization in Rapid City, and then a stroke, all in rapid succession. That was in 1948. For the next two years, he didn't walk but was mostly bedridden—a strange way of living for such a peripatetic man.

There was a wake in the family home. Two of the black robes were there: Father Zimmerman and a young Jesuit named William Siehr. They talked later about how the Northern Lights were more brilliant that night than any they had ever seen before. Siehr, who would himself live another forty years, said, "The sky was just one bright illumination. . . . I never saw anything quite so intense as it was that night."[14] Others said similar things.

Black Elk received a Catholic funeral at St. Agnes Catholic Church in Manderson. He lies there still, on the Pine Ridge Reservation in the tiny Catholic cemetery on a hilltop across the state highway from St. Agnes. A very simple black grave marker reads, "Chief Black Elk." The title "Chief" is likely to be misunderstood. Kathy Cordes, archivist to the Diocese of Rapid City, recently said: "At one of our group meetings, it was explained that the word chief has other meanings to the Lakota. Although never technically a chief—someone who is a leader in the military, designated by rank, etc.—Ben Black Elk, Nicholas' son, and his family bestowed the honor of chief to Nicholas because he was a humble Lakota and because of people's devotion to him."[15] To any Catholic accustomed to the ways of celebrating saints and would-be saints in most locations around the world, the extreme humility of the grave marker and its surroundings will astonish.

His Catholic witness and life of exemplary virtue are being discovered more now than ever before. For instance, a profile in *The New Yorker*, written after Black Elk's cause for canonization was announced in the fall of 2017, returned to the Battle of the Little Bighorn and wondered what the soldiers of the Seventh Cavalry might have been thinking:

> How would General George Custer have responded if he'd been told that one of the greatest American spiritual visionaries of all time was among the Indians he was riding toward and hoping to destroy? What would his troopers—many of them Irishmen, and presumably Catholics—have said if they had been told that one of the children in the Sioux camp would someday be a candidate for sainthood in their church?[16]

CHAPTER ELEVEN

His Afterlife

"Grandfather! Great Spirit!" begins a prayer card recently printed in the Rapid City Diocese of South Dakota. It goes on:

> Behold us, who stand before you, singing our song of thanksgiving for your beloved servant, Nicholas Black Elk.

Today, in the places where Black Elk lived most of his life and did much of his pastoral work—places that exist today as Our Lady of the Sioux Catholic Church in Oglala, St. Agnes Church in Manderson, Holy Rosary Mission/Red Cloud Indian School, and all over the Pine Ridge Reservation—people have long believed in Black Elk's sainthood. That prayer card concludes with this: "Nicholas—pray for us as we open our hearts to recognize the risen Christ in other cultures and peoples, to your glory and honor."[1]

He is credited with bringing at least four hundred people into the Roman Catholic Church, and Pine Ridge today is still filled with Catholics. Without diminishing the difficulty that many people have trying to understand how their ancestor remained both faithfully Lakota and faithfully Catholic, his courage and holiness are unquestioned.

Black Elk experienced the kind of suffering that is often associated with lives of the saints. He expresses this in the interviews he gave, speaking about his people, their losses, their land, and their sorrows. For him, these were also first-hand, tangible losses.

Then there were the sufferings he experienced at home, many of them already mentioned here. His first wife died in 1903, son William died in infancy, son John died of tuberculosis at twelve, an infant son and two stepdaughters died of tuberculosis in 1910. Black Elk himself lived with tuberculosis from at least 1912, at times suffering terribly from it. Then he lost his beloved second wife, Anna, eight years before his own death. But Black Elk never complained about his suffering, and he proclaimed his Catholic faith until the end. "Now my heart is getting sad—but my heart will never turn bad," he wrote in a letter in 1948. "Ever since *Wakan Tanka* (God) gave light to my heart, it stands in light without end."[2]

He is also related to sainthood in the way that he's related to saints who have gone before him. Some people associate a new age spirituality with Native American ideas and practices of living in tune with the rhythms of the earth, but it is easy to see how this is not new agey at all. To be connected to Mother Earth—to use St. Francis of Assisi's famous, forgotten expression—is to be part of the circle of life, honoring the creation of which human beings are only a part. Black Elk understood Mother Earth and the circle of life in the way St. Francis did, and his understanding affected his way of life to the finest detail. Late in life, in teachings of subtle theological depth given to Joseph Epes Brown and translated from Lakota to English by Benjamin Black Elk, Black Elk's son, he offered these prayers:

O Father and Grandfather *Wakan-Tanka*, You are the source and end of everything. My Father *Wakan-Tanka*, You are the One who watches over and sustains all life. O my Grandmother, You are the earthly source of all existence! And Mother Earth, the fruits which You bear are the source of life for the earth peoples. You are always watching over Your fruits as does a mother. May the takes which we take in life upon you be sacred and not weak!

Help us, O *Wakan-Tanka*, to walk the red path with firm steps. May we who are Your people stand in a wakan manner, pleasing to You![3]

All human beings—all Christians—would honor God by doing likewise. Then, when he converted to Catholicism, he added to his worldview the life of the sacraments of the church and an understanding of God as Trinity. The relative seamlessness of this conversion is what has troubled many. To Nick Black Elk, it made perfect sense. And, I suggest, it would have made sense to St. Francis of Assisi, too.

* * *

One Oglala elder, George Looks Twice, started to talk of sainthood for his grandfather decades ago. In 2016, he led the group that sent a petition to their bishop. The petition began:

My name is George Looks Twice, I am an enrolled member of the Oglala Lakota Nation and a member of Our Lady of the Sioux Parish in Oglala, South Dakota, where I was commissioned a Lay Minister for the Rapid City Diocese in 2009. I am the eldest of three grandsons and two granddaughters of the Oglala Holy Man, Chief, and Catechist Nicholas Black Elk.

It is with great honor and privilege to be present on this historical day with my relatives, fellow tribal members, other Native people, priests, and lay ministers from across the diocese to present you with this petition. The petition contains over 1600 signatures from people of goodwill across the United States and Canada. The petition requests that the Diocese of Rapid City proceed as the petitioner to nominate Nicholas Black Elk Sr. for the cause for canonization.[4]

A path of official recognition was also created decades earlier, when the United States Congress and the State of South Dakota created the Black Elk Wilderness Area in 1980—13,000 acres that are sacred to the Sioux and border Mount Rushmore to the south. Black Elk Wilderness Area is part of Black Hills National Forest, an area covering more than 3,100 square miles of southwestern South Dakota and northeastern Wyoming. Then, in the summer of 2016, the US Board on Geographic Names officially renamed Harney Peak—the place the grandfathers took young Black Elk during his important early Great Vision—Black Elk Peak. Black Elk Peak stands 7,242 feet tall and is one of the highest summits east of the Rocky Mountains. It is certainly the tallest mountain in South Dakota.

The renaming of Harney Peak was not without controversy, however. Lakota leader Basil Brave Heart, who lives on Pine Ridge Reservation, suggested the name two years earlier in a letter to the federal board. Brave Heart's reasons seemed obvious: the peak is central to Lakota history and the name Harney is synonymous with the oppression and killing of Lakota people. Army officer William S. Harney was known as an "Indian fighter" throughout his career, particularly between the 1830s and 1850s, for daring and violent raids he led against Seminole, Lakota, and other tribes. He was responsible for killing hundreds of Lakota in Nebraska and South Dakota. Lakota leaders called him "Mad Bear" because Harney would come looking for a fight. Harney was also proslavery and once beat a female slave to death with a stick in St. Louis, Missouri; he faced an inquest and was acquitted. Still, most of the citizens of South Dakota seem to have opposed changing the peak's name. Oral testimony at public hearings indicated this, and a state-appointed name change committee voted to stick with Harney. When the federal board voted unanimously to approve Basil Brave Heart's recommendation, then-Governor Dennis Daugaard, a Republican, opposed it, saying that the state might not support it, perhaps retaining "Harvey Peak" on all its approved travel maps, printed documents, and signs. A week later, the governor acquiesced.

At the November 2017 meeting of the United States Conference of Catholic Bishops in Baltimore, Maryland, Bishop Robert Gruss of Rapid City, South Dakota addressed the gathering on the second day to formally present the cause for canonization of Nicholas Black Elk. This was as expected, as Damian Costello and I had reported a month earlier in an article in *America* magazine:

> Bishop Gruss has decided to continue the process by formalizing the cause for canonization. "The next step is to get the support of the regional bishops, in this case the entire U.S.," he explains. He will bring the matter to the U.S. Conference of Catholic Bishops and expects that his fellow bishops will affirm his findings, as usually happens. He had hoped that this would occur at their June meeting but was unable to get it on the agenda in time; so it will wait until the fall meeting.[5]

One of the more recognized attendees of the November conference, Auxiliary Bishop Robert Barron of the Archdiocese of Los Angeles, wrote about the experience a few days later on his blog. He described Bishop Gruss's "impassioned presentation" and said that the bishops "enthusiastically voted to approve the advancement of Black Elk's cause." Bishop Barron also, then, endorsed Black Elk as "a real icon for catechists in the Catholic Church," hoping that the Native American Catholic might help stop the growth of "nones" and those leaving the church. "Without good catechists, more and more of our young people will fall into secularism and indifferentism," Bishop Barron wrote.[6]

The person to champion a cause for sainthood, gather evidence, interview subjects, compose briefs in support of the cause, is probably the most essential person in the process. In Black Elk's case one of these people (a "vice-postulator") with local roots has been Bill White, who is also an American Lakota Catholic and lay minister. White sees a continuity between Black Elk's spiritual life as a Lakota, expressed as a medicine man, and his Catholicism and work as a catechist.

"I believe God spoke to Black Elk at a very early age, and it isn't likely that this was a message that just came from his village," he said in a recent interview. The content of Black Elk's spiritual vision was continuous from the one to the other, says White: "The message that we must all live in peace and harmony, it was such a Christian concept that it had to have come from God Himself, and it actually informed him and gave him direction for the rest of his life."[7]

Black Elk shows how it is possible to maintain two profound identities at once, for the good of both. We see this, finally, on the subject that is perhaps most essential to Christian teaching and practice—applying what Jesus refers to as one of the two most important teachings of the law. Black Elk said to Lakota Catholics:

In the Bible, Jesus told us that "You should love your neighbor as you love Me." So remember if you get in trouble with your neighbor, remember that God has said, "Love your neighbor." So whatever you have said or if you have done some bad thing to them, go over there and please tell them you are sorry.

And he said to White Americans:

You white people, you come to our country. You came to this country, which was ours in the first place. We were the only inhabitants. After we listened to you, we got settled down. But you're not doing what you're supposed to do—what our religion and our Bible tells us. I know this. Christ himself preached that we love our neighbors as ourself. Do unto others as you would have others do unto you.[8]

There have already been documented cases of miraculous healings accredited to the intercession of Nick. There will surely be more. But only time will tell if the people in the church and the Holy See will come to agree with White, Looks Twice, and others who are already convinced that Nicholas Black Elk is with God.

Acknowledgments

Many thanks to Damian Costello, with whom I wrote the article in *America* that was the genesis of this book. He was too busy promoting the cause of Nicholas Black Elk, as a vice-postulator, to coauthor this with me. I only hope I've done the story justice in his eyes. It would have been better had he written it.

Thank you, too, to Mark G. Thiel, who is also a vice-postulator of the cause, and archivist at the John P. Raynor, SJ, Library at Marquette University in Milwaukee.

My thanks also go to Liturgical Press and Shannon Chisholm, in particular, for appreciating the need to add this biography to their excellent series, "People of God." Stephanie Lancour ushered the manuscript through the process with efficiency. And this book is dedicated to my old friend, Peter Dwyer, the director at Liturgical Press who says he is soon retiring. You will be missed, Peter.

Glossary of Lakota Words and Phrases

Ateunyanpi, "Our Father"

Hehaka Sapa, "Black Elk"

heyoka, "holy fool"

mahpiya, "clouds" (or heaven)

Paha Sapa, "Black Hills"

Sina Sapa, "black robes"

wakan, "holy"

Wakantanka or *Wakan Tanka*, "Great Spirit" (or Holy God)

Wanikiya, "He who makes live" (Jesus)

wasichu, "White people" (literally, "greedy one who takes the fat")[1]

wicasa wakan, "holy man" (or priest)

wichasha wakan, "holy man" (or medicine man)

wocekiye, "church"

Woniya Wakan, "Holy Spirit"

yuwipi, both "healing ceremony" and the "healer/visionary" himself

Notes

Introduction—pages ix–xvii

1. Clyde Holler, ed., *The Black Elk Reader* (Syracuse, NY: Syracuse University Press, 2000), xiii.

2. John G. Neihardt, *Black Elk Speaks: The Complete Edition* (Lincoln, NE: University of Nebraska Press, 2014), 1.

3. *The Song of the Messiah* would be published by Neihardt, via Macmillan, in 1935.

4. I'm not the first to suggest this. Most recently, see Pekka Hämäläinen, *Lakota America: A New History of Indigenous Power* (New Haven, CT: Yale University Press, 2019), 379.

5. Damian Costello, *Black Elk: Colonialism and Lakota Catholicism* (Maryknoll, NY: Orbis Books, 2005), 13.

6. Neihardt, *Black Elk Speaks*, xviii.

7. Nick Estes, *Our History Is the Future: Standing Rock versus the Dakota Access Pipeline and the Long Tradition of Indigenous Resistance* (New York: Verso, 2019), 18.

8. Estes, *Our History Is the Future*, 182.

9. Joe Jackson, *Black Elk: The Life of an American Visionary* (New York: Farrar, Straus and Giroux, 2016), 11.

10. Dick Cavett, "Dr. John Neihardt," DickCavettShow.com, undated remarks, accessed November 14, 2019, https://dickcavettshow.com/index.php/memorable-moments/dr-john-neihardt.

11. Robert M. Utley, *Sitting Bull: The Life and Times of an American Patriot* (New York: Henry Holt, 2008), xv. Utley adds another similarity to the Neihardt case: "Vestal's interpretations of Sitting Bull came as a shock to many Indians and whites identified with his final years" (xv).

12. "Black Elk sainthood cause advances with US bishops' vote," Catholic News Agency/EWTN News, November 17, 2017, https://www .catholicnewsagency.com/news/black-elk-sainthood-cause-advances -with-us-bishops-vote-64152.

Chapter One:
A Place Now Known as Oglala, South Dakota— pages 3–10

1. Quoted in Pekka Hämäläinen, *Lakota America*, 20.
2. Hämäläinen, *Lakota America*, 239.
3. Caroline Fraser, *Prairie Fires: The American Dreams of Laura Ingalls Wilder* (New York: Picador, 2018), 34.
4. Quoted in Fraser, *Prairie Fires*, 56.
5. Jackson, *Black Elk*, 30.
6. Estes, *Our History Is the Future*, 8.
7. Edmund Morris, *The Rise of Theodore Roosevelt* (New York: The Modern Library, 2001), 191; see also 189–97.
8. See Fraser, *Prairie Fires*, 76.
9. Luther Standing Bear, in *Our Hearts Fell to the Ground: Plains Indian Views of How the West Was Lost* (New York: Bedford/St. Martin's, 1996), 125.
10. Henry David Thoreau, *The Journal 1837–1861*, ed. Damion Searls (New York: New York Review Books, 2009), 662.

Chapter Two:
Little Bighorn—pages 11–21

1. Jackson, *Black Elk*, 81.
2. Evan S. Connell, *Son of the Morning Star: Custer and the Little Bighorn* (New York: Harper Perennial, 1985). This is from the caption to the first photograph (no page number).
3. Quoted in Michael A. Elliott, ed., *Custerology: The Enduring Legacy of the Indian Wars and George Armstrong Custer* (Chicago: University of Chicago Press, 2008), 84.

4. Dee Brown, *Bury My Heart at Wounded Knee: An Indian History of the American West* (New York: Holt, Rinehart & Winston, 1970), 289.

5. Neihardt, *Black Elk Speaks*, 53.

6. The Edward Clown Family, as told to William B. Matson, *Crazy Horse: The Lakota Warrior's Life and Legacy* (Layton, UT: Gibbs Smith, 2016), 8.

7. Hämäläinen, *Lakota America*, 7.

8. In Connell, *Son of the Morning Star*, 13. See also Neihardt, *Black Elk Speaks*, 78.

9. Connell, *Son of the Morning Star*, 15.

10. Quoted in Jon Reyhner and Jeanne Eder, *American Indian Education: A History, Second Edition* (Norman, OK: University of Oklahoma Press, 2017), 65.

11. Red Cloud, speech to the secretary of the Interior, *Our Hearts Fell to the Ground*, 154.

12. Quoted by Catherine Denial in "Manifest Destiny: Creating an American Identity," at TeachingHistory.org, https://teachinghistory.org/history-content/ask-a-historian/25502.

13. Quoted by Peter Cozzens in "Ulysses S. Grant Launched an Illegal War Against the Plains Indians, Then Lied About It," *Smithsonian Magazine*, November 2016, https://www.smithsonianmag.com/history/ulysses-grant-launched-illegal-war-plains-indians-180960787/.

Chapter Three:
The Great Vision—pages 22–28

1. Jackson, *Black Elk*, 57–58.

2. Raymond J. DeMallie and Hilda Neihardt, eds., *The Sixth Grandfather: Black Elk's Teachings Given to John G. Neihardt* (Lincoln, NE: Bison Books, 1985), 114.

3. Costello, *Black Elk*, 98.

4. DeMallie, *The Sixth Grandfather*, 116.

5. DeMallie, *The Sixth Grandfather*, 129.

6. DeMallie, *The Sixth Grandfather*, xix.

7. Joseph Epes Brown, editor's preface to *The Sacred Pipe: Black Elk's Account of the Seven Rites of the Oglala Sioux*, recorded and edited by Joseph Epes Brown (Norman, OK: University of Oklahoma Press, 1989), xv.

8. William Stolzman, *The Pipe and Christ: A Christian-Sioux Dialogue* (Chamberlain, SD: Tipi Press, 2002), 74.

Chapter Four:
Indian on Show—pages 29–36

1. Eric Vuillard, *Sorrow of the Earth: Buffalo Bill, Sitting Bull and the Tragedy of Show Business*, trans. Ann Jefferson (London: Pushkin Press, 2016), 25.

2. Vuillard, *Sorrow of the Earth*, 11.

3. Norwegian explorer Johan Adrian Jacobsen; they traveled mostly in Germany. See Wolfgang Haberland, "Nine Bella Coolas in Germany," in *Indians in Europe: An Interdisciplinary Collection of Essays*, ed. Christian F. Feest (Lincoln, NE: University of Nebraska Press, 1989), 337–69.

4. Vuillard, *Sorrow of the Earth*, 12.

5. Hämäläinen, *Lakota America*, 375–76.

6. Neihardt, *Black Elk Speaks*, 135.

7. From *The New York Herald*, November 25, 1886, quoted in Jackson, *Black Elk*, 231.

8. Col. William F. Cody, *The Adventures of Buffalo Bill, 1846–1917* (New York: Harper & Brothers, 1904), 152.

9. Quoted in Rita G. Napier, "Across the Big Water: American Indians' Perceptions of Europe and Europeans, 1887–1906," in *Indians and Europe: An Interdisciplinary Collection of Essays*, ed. Christian F. Feest (Lincoln, NE: University of Nebraska Press, 1999), 384.

10. Jackson, *Black Elk*, 246.

11. Neihardt, *Black Elk Speaks*, 262.

Chapter Five:
The Slaughter at Wounded Knee—pages 37–43

1. Neihardt, *Black Elk Speaks*, 83.

2. Estes, *Our History Is the Future*, 16.

3. Hämäläinen, *Lakota America*, 372.

4. Utley, *Sitting Bull*, 282.

5. Neihardt, *Black Elk Speaks*, appendix, 262.

6. Hämäläinen, *Lakota America*, 378.

7. The Edward Clown Family, *Crazy Horse*, 8.

8. Jackson, *Black Elk*, 331.

9. Cairns Etanhan Wotanin, "Rethinking Wounded Knee," *Lakota Country Times*, April 12, 2018, www.lakotacountrytimes.com/news.

10. Crazy Horse, from *Native American Testimony: A Chronicle of Indian-White Relations from Prophecy to the Present, 1492–1992*, ed. Peter Nabokov (New York: Penguin, 1992), 179.

11. Neihardt, *Black Elk Speaks*, 168.

12. Michael F. Steltenkamp discusses this, while remembering his research, in "Retrospective on *Black Elk: Holy Man of the Oglala*," in Holler, *The Black Elk Reader*, 107.

13. Neihardt, *Black Elk Speaks*, 169.

14. Quoted in Jackson, *Black Elk*, 326.

Chapter Six:
Missionaries and Priests—pages 47–55

1. Charles Eastman, *The Essential Charles Eastman (Ohiyesa): Light on the Indian World*, ed. Michael Oren Fitzgerald (Bloomington, IN: World Wisdom, 2007), 187–88.

2. Jon Reyhner and Jeanne Eder, *American Indian Education: A History, Second Edition* (Norman, OK: University of Oklahoma Press, 2017), 3.

3. Christopher Columbus, *The Four Voyages: Being His Own Log-Book, Letters and Dispatches with Connecting Narratives*, trans. J. M. Cohen (New York: Penguin, 1992), 121, 55–56. It was Columbus who also famously referred to the Native people he met as *Los*

Indios, since he imagined that he had landed in India rather than off the coast of North America.

4. Nabokov, *Native American Testimony*, 50–51.

5. Luther Standing Bear, in *Our Hearts Fell to the Ground*, 125.

6. Quoted in Henry Bowden, *American Indians and Christian Mission* (Chicago: University of Chicago Press, 1981), 188.

7. See George E. Tinker, *Missionary Conquest: The Gospel and Native American Cultural Genocide* (Minneapolis: Fortress Press, 1993), viii.

8. Charles Larpenteur, *Forty Years a Fur Trader on the Upper Missouri: The Personal Narrative of Charles Larpenteur, 1833–1872*, ed. Paul L. Hedren (Lincoln, NE: University of Nebraska Press, 1989), 338, 339–40.

9. This translation was never popular among Lakota speakers, and another was started in the late twentieth century. An article in a South Dakota newspaper in 2008 included: "There are people who disagree that the Bible should be translated into Lakota at all, seeing Christianity as associated with European eradication of Native tribes and cultures." Barbara Soderlin, "Lakota Bible Translation Project Takes Decades," *Rapid City Journal*, September 20, 2008. Available online at https:// rapidcityjournal.com/news/local/lakota-bible-translation-project-takes -decades/article_2cdffbd8-6e95-5047-9b83-26b8e62267e0.html.

10. Hilda Neihardt, *Black Elk and Flaming Rainbow: Personal Memories of the Lakota Holy Man and John Neihardt* (Lincoln, NE: University of Nebraska Press, 1999), 88–89.

11. James R. Walker, *Lakota Belief and Ritual*, ed. Raymond J. DeMallie and Elaine A. Jahner (Lincoln, NE: University of Nebraska Press, 1991), 59.

Chapter Seven:
From Oglala to Rome—pages 56–64

1. Quoted in Costello, *Black Elk*, 22.

2. Interview with Chris Roberts, "Russel Means, in Memoriam," *The Progressive Magazine*, October 24, 2012, https://progressive.org /dispatches/russell-means-memoriam/.

3. Jackson, *Black Elk*, 228.

4. DeMallie, *The Sixth Grandfather*, 14.

5. Michael F. Steltenkamp, *Nicholas Black Elk: Holy Man of the Oglala* (Norman, OK: University of Oklahoma Press, 1993), 33–35.

6. Steltenkamp, *Nicholas Black Elk*, 36.

7. Zitkala-Ša, *American Indian Stories, Legends, and Other Writings*, ed. Cathy N. Davidson and Ada Norris (New York: Penguin, 2003), 236.

8. Damian Costello, "Nicholas Black Elk: Prophet to Lakota a Sign of Hope Today," CatholicPhilly.com, April 15, 2019, https://catholicphilly.com/2019/04/commentaries/nicholas-black-elk-prophet-to-lakota-a-sign-of-hope-today/.

9. For reference: "Today in the United States only 10 to 25 percent of American Indians consider themselves Christians. . . . This estimate hasn't changed in over a century, and the range is maddening for those of us who study religion through a social scientific lens." Jace Weaver, foreword to *Crow Jesus: Personal Stories of Native Religious Belonging*, ed. Mark Clatterbuck (Norman, OK: University of Oklahoma Press, 2017), xii.

10. Costello, *Black Elk*, 9.

11. Steltenkamp, *Nicholas Black Elk*, 91.

12. Costello, *Black Elk*, 77.

Chapter Eight: Catechist Nick—pages 65–76

1. See for instance the statement of the archbishop of Seattle in 1987, in *The Crossing of Two Roads: Being Catholic and Native in the United States*, ed. Marie Therese Archambault, Mark G. Thiel, and Christopher Vecsey (Maryknoll, NY: Orbis Books, 2003), document 74.

2. Stolzman, *The Pipe and Christ*, 181.

3. Quoted in Steltenkamp, *Nicholas Black Elk*, 33.

4. "Petition to Open the Cause for Black Elk Canonization," April 21, 2016, Diocese of Rapid City website, https://www.rapidcitydiocese.org/petition-open-cause-canonization/.

5. Ross Enochs, *The Jesuit Mission to the Lakota Sioux: A Study of Pastoral Ministry, 1886–1945* (Kansas City, MO: Sheed and Ward, 1996), 76.

6. Pope Benedict XV, *Maximum Illud*, November 30, 1919, https://w2.vatican.va/content/benedict-xv/it/apost_letters/documents/hf_ben-xv_apl_19191130_maximum-illud.html.

7. Pope Pius XI, *Rerum Ecclesiae* 27, February 28, 1926, http://w2.vatican.va/content/pius-xi/en/encyclicals/documents/hf_p-xi_enc_28021926_rerum-ecclesiae.html.

8. This is from the letter of 1934 quoted above in chapter 9, but this version includes the Lakota word. See Enochs, *The Jesuit Mission to the Lakota Sioux*, 85.

9. Archambault, Thiel, and Vecsey, *The Crossing of Two Roads*, 134.

10. Archambault, Thiel, and Vecsey, *The Crossing of Two Roads*, 135.

11. Translated and quoted in "Black Elk's Legacy," Mark Thiel, *Whispering Wind*, issue 258, 37, no. 2 (2007): 16.

12. DeMallie, *The Sixth Grandfather*, 23.

13. DeMallie, *The Sixth Grandfather*, 137–38.

14. Raymond Bucko and Kay Koppedrayer, "Father Eugene Buechel's Collection of Lakota Materials," *Material Culture* 39, no. 2 (Fall 2007): 23.

15. Mark G. Thiel, "The Life & Holiness of Nicholas Black Elk, Our Brother in Jesus Christ," Marquette University Archives, 14–15, https://www.marquette.edu/library/archives/documents/NBE4final.pdf.

Chapter Nine:
Baffling Two Communities—pages 77–86

1. William S. Lyon, preface to *Black Elk: The Sacred Ways of a Lakota*, by Wallace Black Elk and William S. Lyon (New York: HarperCollins, 1991), xiii.

2. Black Elk, *The Sacred Pipe*, ed. Brown, xix–xx.

3. V. S. Naipaul, *The Middle Passage: The Caribbean Revisited* (New York: Vintage, 2002), 160.

4. Quotation in Paul B. Steinmetz, *Pipe, Bible, and Peyote among the Oglala Lakota: A Study in Religious Identity* (Syracuse, NY: Syracuse University Press, 1998), 58; as referenced in Enochs, *The Jesuit Mission to the Lakota Sioux*, 85.

5. Jackson, *Black Elk*, 16.

6. Quoted in Ian Frazier, "Another Vision of Black Elk," *The New Yorker*, December 26, 2017, https://www.newyorker.com/news/daily-comment/another-vision-of-black-elk.

7. DeMallie, *The Sixth Grandfather*, 59–61.

8. "Dear Friends," dated September 20, 1934, in *The Crossing of Two Roads*, ed. Archambault, Thiel, and Vecsey, 139–40.

9. Enochs, "Black Elk and the Jesuits," in Holler, *The Black Elk Reader*, 286. Much of this chapter is indebted to this seminal article: see pages 282–301.

10. Enochs, "Black Elk and the Jesuits," in Holler, *The Black Elk Reader*, 282–83.

11. Enochs, "Black Elk and the Jesuits," in Holler, *The Black Elk Reader*, 284.

12. Bishop Joseph F. Busch, ca. 1910–15, in *The Crossing of Two Roads*, ed. Archambault, Thiel, and Vecsey, 121.

13. Enochs, "Black Elk and the Jesuits," in Holler, *The Black Elk Reader*, 294–95.

14. Enochs, "Black Elk and the Jesuits," in Holler, *The Black Elk Reader*, 283.

15. Lucy Looks Twice, quoted in Steltenkamp, *Nicholas Black Elk*, 102. Chap. 7 is devoted to these difficulties of understanding.

16. David Treuer, *The Heartbeat of Wounded Knee: Native America from 1890 to the Present* (New York: Riverhead, 2019), 450.

Chapter Ten:
Quiet Days at Last—pages 89–97

1. "Tuberculosis in indigenous peoples in the U.S., 2003–2008," September/October 2011, Centers for Disease Control and Prevention, Division of Tuberculosis Elimination, Atlanta, https://www.ncbi.nlm.nih.gov/pubmed/21886328.

2. Neihardt, *Black Elk Speaks*, xvii–xix.

3. Jackson, *Black Elk*, 359.

4. Costello, *Black Elk*, 94.

5. Henry Westropp, SJ, "Catechists Among the Sioux," *Catholic Missions* magazine (November 1908): 114.

6. Mark Thiel, "Black Elk's Legacy," *Whispering Wind*, Issue 258, 37, no. 2 (2007): 16.

7. Jackson, *Black Elk*, 379.

8. This is suggested by Jackson, *Black Elk*, 380–81.

9. Mary Claudia Duratschek, *Crusading Along Sioux Trails: A History of the Catholic Indian Missions in South Dakota* (St. Meinrad, IN: Grail, 1947), 207.

10. This is Fr. Zimmerman, quoted in DeMallie, *The Sixth Grandfather*, 61.

11. Quoted in DeMallie, *The Sixth Grandfather*, 65–66.

12. Neihardt, *Black Elk Speaks*, xviii.

13. Jackson, *Black Elk*, 14.

14. Steltenkamp, *Nicholas Black Elk*, 132.

15. Kathy Cordes, "Curia Corner: Servant of God Nicholas Black Elk, Pray for Us," November 20, 2019, Diocese of Rapid City website, https://www.rapidcitydiocese.org/curia-corner-servant-of-god-nicholas-black-elk-pray-for-us/.

16. Frazier, "Another Vision of Black Elk."

Chapter Eleven:
His Afterlife—pages 98–104

1. This is a slight adaptation of the last sentence on the card by Kathy Cordes, "Curia Corner," Diocese of Rapid City website.

2. *Private Letter from Black Elk to Father Gall*, trans. Charlotte Black Elk, March 4, 1948, Marquette University Archives, https://www.rapidcitydiocese.org/wp-content/uploads/2019/08/1948-3-4.pdf.

3. Black Elk, *The Sacred Pipe*, ed. Brown, 14.

4. "Petition to Open the Cause for Black Elk Canonization," Diocese of Rapid City.

5. Damian Costello with Jon M. Sweeney, "Black Elk, the Lakota Medicine Man Turned Catholic Teacher, Is Promoted for Sainthood," *America* magazine, October 1, 2017.

6. Bishop Robert Barron, "Black Elk and the Need for Catechists," Wordonfire.org, November 21, 2017, https://www.wordonfire.org /resources/article/black-elk-and-the-need-for-catechists/5646/.

7. Bill White, interview by Cecily Hilleary, "U.S. Catholics Pursuing Sainthood for Native American Visionary Nicholas Black Elk," *Voice of America*, broadcast December 8, 2017, https://www.voanews.com/a /catholic-church-pursuing-sainthood-for-nicholas-black-elk/4153640 .html?utm_source=dlvr.it&utm_medium=twitter.

8. These two quotations are translations of Michael F. Steltenkamp, found in Damian Costello's "Black Elk Speaks," *William Carey International Development Journal* 3, no. 2 (Spring 2014): 52.

Glossary of Lakota Words and Phrases—page 106

1. This literal definition comes from John Redhouse, introduction, *Wasi'chu: The Continuing Indian Wars*, by Bruce Johansen and Roberto Maestas (New York: Monthly Review Press, 1980), 11.

Index